CAplus-1

(Computer Appreciation plus)

for basic and advance learning

N. Stephen

N. Stephen

CAplus-1

Published By:
Space-Era Data Service,
www.onlineworkdata.com

Printed and Distributes By:
CreateSpace Independent
Publishing Platform,

4900 LaCross Road,
North Charleston, SC 29406, USA

First Edition

ISBN-13:978-1503299559
ISBN-10:1503299554

DEDICATION

This book is dedicated to God Almighty, first for the salvation He gave to me, second for His guidance and third, His provisions in my life. In addition, is to my lovely Mum, Mrs. Nwankwo Grace, a woman of a singular merit and honor, who, though young and beautiful devoted herself entirely to the rearing of my education. May the Almighty God through my Lord Jesus Christ extends her days with divine health. Amen!

THE BOOK CONTENTS

Acknowledgments--- i
Preface-- ii
General Introduction of the Book-- iii

Section-One Content

Section One---------	**Introduction to Computer**------------------------------------	1
	General Introduction of Section-One	2
Chapter One-----	**The History of Computer.**------------------------------------	3
▪ Topic	The Origin of Computer---	4
	Summary list of some Computer Inventors--------------------	12
	Key terminologies and Meanings------------------------------	13
Chapter Two-----	**The Meaning, Uses and Attributes of Computer**------	15
▪ Topic	What is Computer?---	16
▪ "	The Characteristics of computer-----------------------------	19
▪ "	The Uses of Computer--	20
▪ "	The Limitations of Computer---------------------------------	21
	Key terminologies and Meanings------------------------------	22
Chapter Three---	**The Classifications of Computers**------------------------	23
▪ Topic	By Physical Size---	24
▪ "	By Input-Signal System--	32
▪ "	By Architectural Designation---------------------------------	37
▪ "	By Electronic Signal Switch-----------------------------------	40
▪ "	By Microprocessor--	44
▪ "	By Unique Functions---	45
	Key terminologies and Meanings------------------------------	54
Chapter Four----	**The Components of Computer**------------------------------	57
▪ Topic	The Classifications of the Components----------------------	58
▪ "	The Hardware---	59
▪ "	The Software--	61
▪ "	The Disk Drive of a System Unit-----------------------------	65
▪ "	The Computer Storage Device--------------------------------	66
▪ "	Key terminologies and Meanings-----------------------------	67
Chapter Five----	**The Basic Operations of Computer**-- ---------------------	69
▪ Topic	Input-Processing-Output Operations-------------------------	70
▪ "	Input-Processing-Output Devices-----------------------------	73
	Key terminologies and Meanings------------------------------	79
	Practical Activities of Section-One--------------------------	80

Section-Two Content

Section-Two----- **Building Computer Career-**----------------------- 83

General Introduction of Section-Two 84

Career One--- **Information System Manager-**-------------------- 85

Career Two--- **Database Administrator-**-------------------------- 89

Career Three- **Computer Instructor-**------------------------------ 93

Career Four-- **Computer Programmer-**-------------------------- 97

Career Five **Computer Engineering** 103

Key terminologies and Meanings-------------------- 110

Practical Activities for Section-Two---------------- 111

References-- 112

Index-- 115

ACKNOWLEDGMENTS

I acknowledged with a profound gratitude the efforts of my friend, Pastor Beloved Osi, for her sense of commitment and effort in the project. She strongly participated in the grammatical and spelling check of the manuscript. Not to forget is Mr. N. Chris, the Director of Tourch Information Technology Centre (A Subsidiary of Tourch Global Resources Limited) Nigeria and his Students that participated during the index-listing of the book. The Director of LordKel Digital Production, Mr. Kelvin Joseph and his workers for designing the front cover image of the book. Mr. N. Golden for the index-listing work, and everyone whose material contributed as reference to the book. Lastly, people like Mr. George Urim, Rev. C. Elijah, Rev. A. William, Dr. Kalu I. Emele, Mr. Samuel Osi, Mr. Nnamdi Ukpabi, Mrs. Emmanuel Favour, Mr & Mrs. Amugo Kalu, Ms. Favour Godwin, and Mr. Chuka Osi who prayed and encouraged me irrespective of distance.

PREFACE

As most people know, the World has gone into a technological revolution. In the forefront of this revolution is an electronic machine with superlative functions, and capabilities in the application of works of lives. The impact analysis of this 'machine' shows that its available programs and services are multiplying every day, therefore all aspect of human activities ranging from learning and communication practices, marketing, information searching, research works, business transactions, social networking, medical services, and others are presently engulfed with it. So the use of the machine is at exponential increase in order to enable this present generation improved on works of lives. But, ignorance has denied many people the knowledge of this great machine, known as 'computer'. Although, not in all countries, as the case is in some *More Developed Countries (MDCs)*, but to some regions of the World like the *Less Developed Countries (LDCs)* were the appreciation and learning is not intensive. Truly, there is a large computer-knowledge-gap between those living with the knowledge, and those who have not appreciate the knowledge, and this therefore, calling the need for computer appreciation, not only to LDCs, but also to some members of MDCs.

The term *"Computer Appreciation"* was coined by Richard W. Hamming (circa 1960) when he indicated the need for broad scale education about computers (Arthur B. Kahn, 1967)[1]. In other words, Hamming advocacy emphasized on the need to expand the learning of computer in order to improve the course of education scale, especially in countries where there is such need. So to achieve this objective, people have to begin the learning of computer in order to sharpen their future, which is partly framed in computer technology. They must in their various facets of works embrace the trend by being computer literate so that the future generation will inherit a good work done for the society.

Supportively, **CAplus (KA+)** is part of the solution. It is a written work for basic and advance learning of computer, and are in ***book-one, two, three, and four*** format. The author who has more than 16 years computing experience as of when it was written made an intensive gathering of knowledge together with his experience to write about it, within a period of 3-4 years. The **'plus'** added to the name (i.e. computer appreciation plus) indicates that the books are more than a mere computer appreciation book. The basic part of the books are written to serve as the first step for computer learning beginners, which included those at the tertiary level, pupils in secondary schools, and private individuals who are professionals in various areas of works. And the advance part is to support the computer application knowledge of the intermediate and advance computer users. The author welcomes the general public for the uses of the books.

N. Stephen

November 2014.

1. Arthur B. Kahn stated this in his book titled "An Appreciation of Computer Appreciation. Published in ACM New York, NY, USA, 1967.

GENERAL INTRODUCTION OF THE BOOK

By computer appreciation, we are referring to the technology impart of understanding computer through learning and practicing the first-step of its composition, scope, and operations in ICT World. This is for basic, but for advance computer appreciation, it is to support the computer application knowledge of the intermediate and advance computer users, who perform their daily activities with computer.

By comparison, appreciation is different from "computer application", which is the technical impart of understanding how to use application programs of computer through practice. In other words, the key difference between both of them is that the capability attachment of the later (computer application) depends on the former (computer appreciation). Meaning that the ability to perform effectively in computer application depends on the knowledge gained from the computer appreciation. Following this point, the general objectives of this book-one are to help users gain and improve in both computer appreciation and application. At the end of the study, students would achieve the followings:

- complete historical, meaning, attributes, and classifications knowledge of computer;
- basic and advance operating system knowledge of computer;
- know the common hardware and software components of computer; and
- can be able to instruct or teach basic computer appreciation course;

To gainfully cover these objectives, the book was written in sections, and each section consists of various chapters, key terminologies, practical, and online references.

For the content, *Section-One* contains chapter one to five with the topics on history of computer, the meaning, attributes and uses of computers, including the classifications of computer, common components basic operations of computer relatively. It runs to counter the myth-belief that many people have over computer. This is because many never accept the nature of computer as not being a voodoo machine. The limitations of computer are still in doubt, and the ability to identify any machine that belongs to the families of computers is not yet clarified to some people. In addition, the last chapter emphasized on how computer carries out its common operations such as input-processing-output functions in relation to its various components.

Section-Two is titled "building computer career" theme, which comprises six examples of computer career topics, with cases of teaching students on how to build and enhance computer careers through educational system, participatory in application program training, and relative software to each specialized area of the career. For instance, a topic was taught based on the best software and guidelines that computer science career person has to undergo in order to realize the goals of the career.

However, for complete benefit-effectiveness, it is advisable to use both **CAplus-1, 2, 3, and 4**. So **CAplus-2** was written for advance-level in order to help students in the studying of computer's components. To support its central teaching, the book explained the hardware and software components of the computer, and how they function systematically in the work process of computation. In this form, the knowledge-gained about these components goes a long way to assist students in learning computer maintenance and repair, troubleshooting identification, and how to manage computer threats, which are the central teaching in **CAplus-4**.

For the CAplus-3, the general study of computer appreciation is not complete without the introduction of computer application, and since Windows Operating System (OS) is the main OS in the work of CAplus, therefore "windows appreciation" was written in **CAplus-3** as a prepared take-off ground for computer application training. To widen the book, the concept of file, and folder were treated, including topics on "internet appreciation", "computer threats appreciation", and "system quality assurance analysis." The internet appreciation is to teach students the intricate of internet browsing. The computer threats appreciation is to expose students gain knowledge about the enemy of computer application, i.e. virus and malware, and the system quality assurance analysis is to enhance learners on how to analyse the quality of computer.

Some Key Terms

*AC/DC
*Application Software
*Batch
*Buffer
*CPU
*Database
*DASD
*Giga byte (GB)
*Graphic
*Hardware
*HTTP
*IEEE 802.11 standards
*INTEL
*Interface
*Interoperability
*Kilo byte (KB)
*Megabyte (MB)
*Open Group
*Open Software Standard
*Open source
*Operating System (OS)
*Palm OS
*Precision
*Parallel Sysplex
*Real time
*Serialization
*Sexagismal Number System
*Terabyte (TB)
*Terminal
*Virtual machines
*Wi-Fi
*Window CE
*Workstation

SECTION-ONE
Introduction to Computer

Section Studies

The Section studies are grouped in the following chapters:

1. Chapter One-The History of Computer

2. Chapter Two-The Meaning, Uses and Attributes of Computer

3. Chapter Three-The Classifications of Computers

4. Chapter Four-The Components of Computer

5. Chapter Five-The Basic Operations of Computer

Practical Activities

There are listed series of practical activities for the Section.

Objectives of the Studies

At the end of the study, Students should be able to:

- understand the chronological origin of computer;
- know the countries and individuals who played vital roles in the inventions of computers;
- mention and describe various types of computer developed within the passage of time;
- know the meaning of computer;
- understand the uses, characters and limitations of computer in carrying out its functions;
- know the different classification of computer;
- know the components of computer, and how computer runs its basic operations.

GENERAL INTRODUCTION OF SECTION-ONE

Before the early 1980s, in the region of Developing Countries like Nigeria, Ghana, Algeria, Sudan, Palestine and other developing countries, computer as an electronic machine was less known despite its popularity in Developed Countries like some European Countries, USA, Japan and some other parts of Asian continent. It was then seen as a spiritual machine that can perform all form of superlative works. For instance, many less developed people hearing its superlative functions often considered it (computer) as a mysterious machine that has mystical forces attached to those functions. Some went a long way believing it is the work of 'voodoo'. So as of these periods, no notable individual owns computer except some large institutions. However, with reference to the passage of time, relating to technological advancement and modernization, which took place in Europe and USA within the period of 1970s-1980s, the awareness of computer existence, uses, and important took over the African region (as the case was in Nigeria). But, this time, it was no longer seen as a mysterious machine, but rather a complex and expensive machine, which is only made to the ownership of rich private individuals and organizations. But, today, about many thousands of companies, institutions of learning and as well as private individuals own computers. For example, an average household in Nigeria, South Africa, and other part of African countries can afford a personal computer (PC). This is because technological advancement and manufacturing competition have reduced the retail prices, and its applications are needed in all spheres of human endeavours and works of lives. All human activities are computerized, and computer is now realized as a device, which can enable man perform his daily activities at a faster rate.

So in this Section-One, which comprises Chapter one to five, we made an attempt to explain in a large extent, the history, meaning, classifications and other parts of this mysterious machine called computer. And at the end of the Chapters, students are expected to achieve the aforementioned objectives of this Section stated on the page.

Chapter One of Section-One

The History of Computer

INTRODUCTION

The invention of computer began thousands years ago, and this covered different eras and generations. In tracing the history and grouping of the inventions, we can use different approaches, for example, we can emphasize on the exact types of invented computers like Abacus, and ENIAC based on dates of their inventions, or generally grouped them into various technological existences such as stone, mechanical, mechanical-electrical and, electrical-electronic eras. We can also explain them based on generational passage of time. Now, in this book, we adopted a historical approach framed on types of computer technology that have existed, and their generational passage of time. So we track the inventions of computers based on ascending orders of dates and, classified the eras into mechanical and electronics inventions periods of computer, relatively to general passage of time. To achieve the chapter objectives, the author took time to research plenty online articles and eBooks in the preparation of the chapter, and therefore encourages students, especially those whose career background is on information technology to know the historical background of the machine.

THE ORIGIN OF COMPUTER

The origin of computer invention began from the struggle of man to solve mathematical or computation problems. In this, the first form of computer was human being. For instance, before the thirteen century, computers (also called *computors*) were human clerks that performed human computations. As of then, many thousands of these computors were employed in commerce, government, and research establishments. Most of them were women, and they that have degrees in calculus and statistics. To some extent, most of them performed astronomical calculations for calendars. So they were employed to do calculations involved in works. But, due to boredom and human error in calculation, therefore, there was the need for another form of computor, which is preferable to be a machine and not human being, so this led to the invention of the first computer known as Abacus. Since emerging of abacus as the earliest computing object, there is an argument over who or country that invented it (abacus) first.

An abacus (plural abaci or abacuses), also called a counting frame is a calculating tool for performing arithmetical processes, often constructed as a wooden frame with beads sliding on wires. The first abacus was mostly look like a flat stone covered with sand or dust, and letters were drawn on the sand. But, eventually numbers were added and pebbles that are used to aid calculations. Though, this feature has made some Babylonian Scholars believing that abacus was first used in Babylon as early as 2400 BCE before any other place in the world. The Babylonians in this period were known to have used an object called *cuneiform*, which can as well function like Abacus. But, following the Mesopotamian historical records, the period of 2700-2300 BCE saw the first appearance of the *Sumerian* abacus. The Sumerian abacus was a table of successive columns that delimited the successive orders of magnitude of their sexagesimal number system. Supportively, this is in aligned with the Babylonians' claim, since they are Sumerians. On the contrariwise, some scholars have attributed credit to the Chinese community as the first inventor of the device. Although, no matter who invented the device first, many countries developed variety of abaci, these include Greek abacus, Egypt, Japanese, and Russian abacus.

The Babylonian Cuneiform

THE MECHANICAL ERA (2400 BC-1938 AD)

Abacus became the first mathematical calculating object, and then in 1195 BCE, the South Point Chariot (SPC) was invented in China. The SPC was a gear mechanism machine used for gear differentiation. With time, the Chinese also invented a more sophisticated Abacus known as Chinese Abacus in the 2nd century BCE. Then, in 1901, computer known as Antikythera mechanism was discovered by sponge divers who chanced upon the shipwreck of a Roman vessel, off the coast of the Greek Island of Antikythera. The Antikythera mechanism was the earliest mechanical analog computer, and was designed to calculate astronomical positions.

Although, before the discovery of Anthikythera mechanism in 1901, the Islamic world with their Mathematicians, Engineers and Astronomers have done great works in computer invention, especially in the area of inventing mechanical analog computers. For example, Abū Ibrāhīm, an Islamic Spain (*circa* 1015) developed Equatorium mechanical analog computer used as astro-meteorological calculating instrument. Then other analog mechanical computers and their inventors were Torquetum invented by Jabir ibn Aflah. The Torquetum is used to take and convert measurements made in three sets of coordinates: horizon, equatorial, and ecliptic. The "castle-clock", an astronomical clock invented by Al-Jazari in 1206, and was considered to be the earliest programmable analog computer used for zodiac, solar, and checking of the day and night, and length, which could be re-programmed to compensate for the changing lengths of day and night throughout the year.

Following with the passage of time, also before that 1901 of Antikythera mechanism discovery, in early17th century, Wilhelm Schickard in 1623 constructed the first mechanical calculator, although the device did not fit the modern definition of computer because it was not programmable. In the same 17th century, a Scottish Mathematician named John Napier developed a logarithm tables for arithmetic calculations. Furthermore, in 1642, Blaise Pascal, a French Mathematician developed the first mechanical calculator called Pascaline, which was used for mathematical calculation. Then, in 1671, a German mathematician named Gottfried Von Leibniz developed the first calculator for multiplication as well as other simple arithmetic calculations.

In 1801, Joseph Marie Jacquard, a French Engineer developed a loom known as Jacquard Loom, which is a punched board system for Power Looms. The punched board system was used automatically in designing specific weaving patterns on cloths. For advancement, the resulting Jacquard loom was an important step in the development of computers. This is because the use of punched cards to define woven patterns can be viewed as an early, although limited, but form of programmability in computer invention. But, this brought the concept of programmability, which led to the fusion of automatic calculation, and production of the first recognizable computers. So later, the idea of punched boards was adopted and used in developing calculation devices. From this, in 1820, a French scientist called Charles Xavier invented a calculating machine named Arithmometer that could perform simple arithmetic calculations such as addition, subtraction, multiplication, and division.

Jacquard Loom, 1801

Following the trend, in 1823 to 1837, Professor Charles Babbage at Cambridge University of UK developed a special type of calculator called "*Difference Engine*", which was powered by steam for mathematical calculations. The Difference Engine's arithmetic capability was limited, but it could compile and print mathematical tables with no more human intervention than a hand to turn the handles at the top of the device. Although the British Government was impressed enough to invest £17,000 in the construction of a full-scale of it, but, it was never built. So the project came to a halt in 1833 in a dispute over payments between Babbage and his workmen. Progressively, in 1842, Babbage also designed a new machine called the "*Analytical Engine*", which was the first automatic programmable computer.

The Analytical Engine had all the essential parts of the modern computer, for example, the means of entering a set of instructions, a memory, a central processing unit (CPU), and a means of outputting results. For input and programming, Babbage made it possible with the used of punched cards, which is an idea that he borrowed from Joseph Jacquard, who had used them in his revolutionary weaving loom in 1801. Although, the Analytical Engine's average speeds to perform arithmetic calculations was 60 additions per minute. However, in 1853, George Scheutz and his son Edward Scheutz modified Charles Babbage Difference Engine to develop a machine that calculates a 15 digit numbers.

But, between the periods of 1882-1890, an American scientist named Herman Hollerith used the idea of the Jacquard loom and introduced the punched cards as input media in computer. He developed the first electro-mechanical punched cards tabulator. This machine could read information that had been punched into cards as the cards were maintained in stack form. So this brought solutions to different problems whereby information could be stored on different stacks of cards and accessed when needed, therefore, marks the beginning of data processing and storage.

As time goes on, in 1890, the Herman Hollerith punched card machines were used by USA Census Bureau for their 1890 census with the technical assistance of the Hollerith company that later became the core of International Business Machine (IBM) in 1924.

In contribution for the furtherance of more computers due the invention of the Hollerith tabulator, then from 1926-1935, the D11 tabulator was invented in Germany by DEHOMAG (Deutsche Hollerith Maschinen Gesellschaft), which is a German subsidiary of IBM with monopoly in the Nazi market during World War II. The D11 was capable of multiplying, dividing, and direct balancing. It could also punch results into punch cards. Its control panel provided the means to mechanize large and complex processing.

The Hollerith Tabulator, 1882

The Analytical Engine, 1842

However, with time from 1936 to 1938, Konrad Zuse, being recognized in Germany as the father of computer, and seen as the inventor of the program-controlled computer, developed a programmable automaton machine that is called Z1, which is the world's first programmable calculating machine. Progressively, around 1938, he (Zuse) began a work on the creation of the Plankalkul, which is the first fully-fledged algorithmic programming language as he was working on the Z3.

Later, during the war years in Berlin, he built the Z4, which is a relay (an electrically operated switch) computer with a mechanical memory of unique design. The Z4 was used for numerical analyses as it was been discovered in 1949 in Bavaria by Eduard Stiefel, who was a professor at the Swiss Federal Institute of Technology (ETH).

THE ELECTRONIC ERA (1937-2010)

The electronic era is classified into various generational periods. The era emerged due to the inventions of the punch cards, which opened a way for modern data processing. So IBM and other computer manufacturers came in this field and began the manufacturing of computers that could use punched cards to run input-processing-output functions, including memory storage. So with the feature of in-built data input program, these computers were able to perform arithmetic calculations and sort numbers. Although they were slow in data processing because each of them can only process 50-220 cards per minute, and each card has a limit of 80 bits (a bit is a single digit in base 2, e.g. 1 or 0). So to enhance the weakness of the punch cards, which is the featured slowness in processing of input data, computer inventors moved and developed computers characterized with vacuum tubes, transistors and integrated circuits.

The First Generation of the Electronic Era (1936-1953)

Briefly about Alan Turing, he is widely regarded to be the father of modern computer science. For instance in 1936, he provided an influential formalization of the concept of algorithm and computation to aid computer invention, therefore computers bearing the formalization of Alan Turing were seen as *Turing machines*. However, Turing machines are not intended as a practical computing technology, but rather as a thought experiment representing a computing machine. The fact remains that in today's computer operation, anyone who taps at a keyboard, opening a spreadsheet or a word-processing program, is working on the incarnation of *Turing machine*. Progressively, as of 1943, Turing also designed computer called *Colossus*; a special-purpose electronic computer designed for deciphering of German codes that was to be used by the British military during the Second World War.

Moreover, in-between the years of 1936-1943 that Alan Turing did his works, many computers were invented by others. For instance, within that period (i.e. between 1936-1943), in the year of 1937; George Stibitz developed the first international recognized digital computer, therefore gained an international recognition as the father of the modern digital computer by building a relay-based calculator. Though, most computers developed this era were using electronic switches in the form of vacuum (electron) tubes, instead of relays.

So the earliest form of vacuum tube computer was built from 1939 to 1942 by Dr. John Atanasoff, a professor of Iowa State University, USA and his assistant, Clifford Berry. In joint hand, Atanasoff and Berry designed an electronic machine called *Atanasoff-Berry Computer (ABC)* that solves mathematical problems of simultaneous equation of 29 unknown variables. But, the computer, although not programmable made was built with 45 vacuum tubes used for performing internal logic operation, capacitor for data storage, and Boolean algebra (algebra of logic) was applied for designing the circuits of it.

Then, in 1944, Mark-1 known as ASCC (Automatic Sequence Controlled Calculator) was developed by an American named Dr. Howard Aiken, who was a professor in Harvard University, USA. Mark-1 was used in solving complex mathematical problems.

In 1946, computer known as ENIAC (Electronic Numerical Integrator And Calculator) was developed by J.P. Eckert and J. Mauchly at the Moore School of Engineering, University of Pennsylvania in USA. The periodical years of developing ENIAC, took place from 1943 to 1946, and the computer was seen as the first programmable electronic computer. It contained about 18,000 vacuum tubes and was programmed by physically connecting of electrical wires in the proper order. It was very difficult to operate, to detect errors and to change the program, but, it could store and manipulate limited amount of data.

To enhance their work, both Eckert and Mauchly in 1952 developed another computer called UNIVAC (Universal Automatic Computer), and John Von Neumann, a Hungarian-born American mathematician, noticing the ENIAC problem in changing program, proposed the concept of the stored program—that is, the technique of coding the program in the same way. So in 1953, he developed EDVAC (Electronic Discrete Variable Automatic Computer), which was used, to stored programs and performs arithmetic and logical operations.

Then, within these periods of 1952-1953, IBM Corporation introduced the 701 commercial computers. After this, came an improved model of the UNIVAC and other IBM 700-series machine models. Rightly in 1953, they (IBM) also produced the IBM-650 computer, IBM 709 (in 1959), and sold over 1000 of these computers.

The Second Generation (1954-1962)

In this period, as a result of technology transition in computer inventions relatively to the previous development and designs of the most of the invented computers, therefore transistor computers emerged. These computers were characterized with several important developments at all levels of computer system designations. For example, from the technology used of building of the basic circuits, and to the programming languages used in writing scientific applications. Though, electronic switches in this era were based on discrete diode and transistor technology development form. So programming languages got a place. Good examples of them are FORTRAN Programming Language developed in 1956 by John Backus, ALGOL (1958), and COBOL (1959).

For the invention of transistor computers; the University of Manchester's experimental Transistor Computer manufactured by Semiconductor Test Consortium (STC) was first operational in November 1953, and it is widely believed by some people as the first transistor computer to come into operation anywhere in the world.

Although, the Computer required some vacuum tubes to produce a clock pulse at its fast speed of 125KHz, so it was not the first *fully* transistorized computer as many argued. Others are TRADIC developed at Bell Laboratories in 1954, which is a laboratory research transistor digital computer designed to explore the capabilities of new solid state devices for airborne computers. In addition, Harwell CADET, which was the first operated transistor computer in 1955, although, it operated on low speed level.

Furthermore, from 1955 to 1959, computers like ETL-Mark 2, JUJIC, MUSASINO-I, ETL-Mark-4, PC-1, ETL-Mark-4a, TAC, Handai-Computer and K-1 were built in Japan. Although, most of them were experimental computers designed and produced by Japanese national laboratories, universities and private companies, so there was still search on how to develop computer with a higher processing speed.

The Third Generation (1963-1972)

For further search of computer with a higher processing speed, the device called integrated circuit (IC) were then included in the developing of computers. IC is a semiconductor device with several transistors built into one physical component. Other features needed are semiconductor memories, microprogramming to support complex processor, and the introduction of operating system and timesharing, which is the sharing of computing resource among many users by means of multi-programming and multi-tasking.

So in 1964, Digital Equipment Corporation (DEC) manufactured PDP-8, which was the first true minicomputer. Although, this was the same year Seymour Cray developed the CDC 6600 (Computer Data Corporation 6600), which was the first recognized supercomputer that could attain a computation of a million floating point operations per second (Mflops).

In this manner, floating point operations are mostly addition, subtraction, and multiplication with enough digits of precision to model systematic computation for continuous phenomena such as weather. This was for instance, to enable weather forecasting through computer computation.

Then in 1966, IBM 1360 Photostore-online terabit mass storage computer was developed. In reaching to 1969, Seymour also developed CDC 7600, which was the first vector processor that can execute 10 million floating-point operations per second. Though, there other computers developed in these periods that are not mentioned.

Furthermore, since the period included the development of programming languages, then in 1970 Ken Thompson of Bell Labs developed yet another simplification of Combined Programming Languages (CPL) called Simply Basic, which is in connection with an early implementation of the UNIX operating system (OS). But, before this development, in 1963, Cambridge University, and the University of London cooperated in the development of CPL. CPL was, according to its authors, an attempt to capture only the important features of the complicated and sophisticated ALGOL. Similarly, CPL been like ALGOL was large with many features that were hard to learn. So in an attempt to simplify it, Martin Richards of Cambridge in 1967 developed a subset of it (CPL) called BCPL (Basic Computer Programming Language), and in 1970, came that of Ken Thompson CPL.

The Fourth Generation (1972-1984)

Since the need of improving computer invention also involve attaining a high processing speed rate, so from 1971 to 1984, the Small Scale Integration (SSI) was improved into Large Scale Integration (LSI) and Very Large Scale Integration (VLSI) with 1000 and 100,000 devices per chip respectively, therefore there was an improvement in the processing speeds of computer. In addition to this processing speed improvement, the built of computers were made simplified in the making that the processor, main memory, and input/output controls could fit into a single integrated circuit.

How this took place is that, within these periods, for in 1972, Dennis Ritchie and Thompson B developed the C-Language from the design of the CPL. Then with time, both of them used C-language to write a version of UNIX for the DEC PDP-11. As result of this, in 1978, DEC introduced VAX11/780 supercomputer, although, there are others that are not mentioned. But, following this advancement, in 1981, the Microsoft Corporation., and International Business Machines (IBM) introduced the first Personal Computers (PCs), which we are using today. The PC was built under the Microsoft Disking Operating System (MS DOS). The major contributors were Bill Gate, Paul Allen and Tom Paterson. Then, in 1983, the first Microsoft Window (MS Window) was developed and announced.

The Fifth Generation (1984-1990)

This period involves the introduction of some new features and improvement of the existing features. From 1984 to the period of 1990, the existing computers were developed with the introduction of the following features:

- with hundreds processors that could all be working on different parts of a single program;

- an increase in the scale of integration, for example, in 1990, it was possible to build chips with a million components;

- standardization of semi-conductor memories in all computer;

- popularity of computer networks and single-user workstations;

- the introduction of parallel processing (computation of multiple operations or tasks simultaneously) and rapid development of WAN (Wide Area Network) and LAN (Local Area Network);

- improvement in programming programs; and

- formula invention of faster internet computer calculation.

Furthermore, some of the computers developed at this period were Sequent Balance 8000, sequent balance 21000 developed by computer company called Sequent in 1984, and SIMD (Single Instruction, Multiple Data) computers. The Sequent Balance 8000 is computer that connects up to 20 processors to a single shared memory module, as each processor has its own local cache, which is a temporary holding data storage place for a single device. It was widely used to explore parallel algorithms and programming techniques. The SIMD was built with several thousand simple processors, which work under the direction of a single control unit. One of examples of SIMD computer is GAPP (Geometric-Arithmetic Parallel Processor), invented by a Polish mathematician named Włodzimierz Holsztyński in 1981.

Then in 1989, an additional invention to aid the uses of computer was made by the Gordon Bell Prize, via a Nobel Prize award winner of 1989 named Philip Emeagwali, who is regarded as one of the fathers of supercomputer and Internet pioneer. This is because he invented the formula that used 65,000 separate computer processors to perform 3.1 billion calculations per second, which made him to be the pioneer of international network that is predates as 'Internet'. This led to the reinvention of some new supercomputers and as well new dimension in internet world. He also discovered mathematical equations that could enable the petroleum industry to recover more oil through the use of computer.

The Sixth Generation (1990-2013)

The period of 1990 to 2010 covered the improvements of the most introduced features. So in this period, there was the improvement of most functions of computer, such as:

- Workstation technology continued to improve, with processor designs now using a combination of RISC (reduced instruction set computing), pipelining (a set of data processing elements connected in series, so that the output of one element is the input of the next one) and parallel processing.

- WAN, network bandwidth and speed of operation and networking capabilities have kept developing tremendously.

- Personal computers (PCs) now operate with Gigabit per second processors, multi-Gigabyte disks, hundreds of Megabytes of (Random Access Memory), colour printers, high-resolution graphic monitors, stereo sound cards and graphical user interfaces. In addition, is the development of more application software and improvement of operating system software, which are the bedrock of task performances in computers. For example, operating systems like Windows 95, Windows 2000, Windows 2005, Windows 7, Windows 8, and Vista are commonly for PCs. While Linux is commonly for Supercomputers and, Mac OS X is for Macintosh computers. In addition are application software like MS Word, MS Excel, MS PowerPoint, MS Outlook, etc.

- The improvement of most application software versions for better performances.

The Participated Countries in Computer Inventions

By records, hundreds of people from different countries of the world played prominent roles in this history of computer. The major countries are the Islamic world comprising of Iraq and others, China, India, British, USA, France, Germany, Japan, and Nigeria.

Summary List of Some Computer Inventors

Years	Inventors	Name and Form of Computers
2700-2300 BC	Sumerians	Cuneiform (or Sumerian Abacus)
1195 BCE	Chinese People	South Point Chariot, a gear mechanism machine used for gear differentiation.
1015 (circa)	Abū Ibrāhīm	Equatorium analog computer, used as astrometeorological calculating instrument.
1206	Al-Jazari	Castle-clock, a programmable analog computer used for checking zodiac and solar activities.
1623	Wilhelm Schickard	A mechanical calculator for arithmetic usage.
1671	Gottfried Von Leibniz	A simple Arithmetic calculator
17th Century	John Napier	Computer for arithmetic calculation
1642	Blaise Pascal	Pascaline and Arithmetic Calculator
1671	Gottfried V.L	The first full functional calculator
1801	J.M Jacquard	Jacquard Loom used in the design and weaving of cloths.
1820	Charles Xavier	Computer that calculates all forms of arithmetic.
1823	Charles Babbage	Difference Engine for mathematical calculation.
1842	Charles Babbage	An Analytical Engine that runs as an automatic programming computer.
1882-1890	Herman Hollerith	The first electro-mechanical punched cards tabulator.
1901	Discovered in Greece	Antikythera, a mechanical analog computer, designed to calculate astronomical positions.
1936	Konrad Zuse	Z1, a programmable automaton machine.
1937	George Stibitz	The first Digital computer.
1938	Konrad Zuse	Z3, an algorithmic programming language
1940s	Konrad Zuse	Z4 used for numerical analysis
1942	J. Atanasoff and C. Berry	*Atanasoff-Berry Computer, used for* mathematical problems of simultaneous equation.
1943	Alan Turing	Colossus, a special-purpose electronic computer designed for German codes deciphering.
1944	Howard Aiken	Mark-1, known as Automatic Sequence Controlled Calculator (ASCC).
1946	J.P Eckert and J. Mauchly	ENIAC (Electronic Numerical Integrator And Calculator)
1952	J.P Eckert and J. Mauchly	UNIVAC (Universal Automatic Computer)
1953	John Von Neumann	EDVAC (Electronic Discrete Variable Automatic Computer)
1953	IBM	IBM-650, a vacuum commercial computer.
1953	University of Manchester	University of Manchester's experimental Transistor Computer.
1954	Bell Laboratories	TRADIC, designed explore the capabilities of new solid state devices for airborne computers.
1955	University of Manchester	Harwell CADET, the first operated transistor computer in 1955.
1956	John Backus	FORTRAN Programming Language
1959	IBM	IBM 709, a vacuum commercial computer.
1959	Japanese People	Handai, TAC, ETL-Mark-4 Compute, etc.
1964	DEC	PDP-8, the first minicomputer.
1964	Seymour Cray	CDC 6600, the first supercomputer.
1970	Ken Thompson	Basic Computer Programming Language
1973	Micral N.	Micral, the first microprocessor Personal Computer
1975	Ed. Roberts and Co.	MITS Altair 8800, the first commercialized microcomputer.
1978	DEC	VAX11/780, a supercomputer.
1981	IBM and Microsoft Corporation	PCs (Personal Computers)
1989	Philip Emeagwali	The formula to run supercomputer and internet speed rate

End of Chapter One of Section-One

Key Terminologies and Meanings

Terms	Meaning
Bit	It is the smallest storage space, for any storage devices usually in binary digit. In other words, it is a single digit in base 2. For example, 1 or 0.
Byte	A group of digital bits, whereby 8 bits make a byte.
Cache	A special block of fast memory used for the storage of temporary data for quick retrieval. In other words, it is a temporary holding data storage place for a single device.
CPL	It means Computer Programming Languages. They are computers acceptable program writing languages. Examples, FORTRAN, ALGOL, and COBOL.
FLOPs	It means *Floating Point Operation Per Second*. It mostly addition, subtraction, and multiplication with enough digits of precision to model continuous phenomena such as weather.
Integrated Circuit	It is a single physical component, which constitutes several transistors.
Interleave	This is to arrange data in a non-contiguous way in order to increase performances. When used to describe disk drives, it refers to the way sectors on a disk are organized. For example, one-to-one interleaving, two-to-one interleaving.
Memory	Refer as a space, which serves as a temporary storage for programs and data in computer
Multi-tasking	It is the ability to carry out multiple operations or tasks simultaneously by executing instructions from multiple different programs.
Network	It is the connection of a group of computers together with cable. At this point, the computers share both some software and hardware together.
Parallel processing	It is the ability to carry out multiple operations or tasks simultaneously. In other words, it is the simultaneous use of more than one CPU or processor core to execute a program or multiple computational threads.
Peripheral	It is all physical components of computer.
RAM	Known as Random Access Memory. It is a temporal storage device where the program and data used in the computer are stored when the computer is switched 'on'.
Relay	A relay is an electrically operated switch
Sexagesimal Number System	A numeral system with sixty as its base.
Software	It is a set of programs designed by computer programmers telling computer on how to perform some tasks.
Transistor	It is a semiconductor device used to amplify and switch electronic signals, but made of a solid piece of semiconductor material.
Vacuum Tube	It is an electron tube device used to amplify, switch and create an electrical signal by controlling the movement of electrons in a low-pressure space.

Objectives Assessment of Chapter One

1. Examine yourself whether you perfectly achieved the objectives of this last Chapter, if not, read it again. However, if you have any question regarding to what you have learnt, visit **www.onlineworkdata.com**.

2. If you are successful, move to the next Chapter;

   "The Meaning, Uses and Attributes of Computers"

Chapter Two of Section-One

The Meaning, Uses and Attributes of Computer

INTRODUCTION

Understanding the meaning and possessing the ability to express the characters of a modern computer are necessary and sufficient in the application and studying of computer course. But, to choose a suitable definition is not an easy task. This is because various forms of computers with different functions and sizes had been invented. So many individuals and institutes have defined and expressed the 'machine' according to the way they understood. For instance, in this Chapter, we will take a look at the various expressed definitions of computer by different individuals, and characters of a modern computer. Though, by modern computer, we are referring to digital computers.

WHAT IS COMPUTER?

The first used of the word 'computer' was recorded in 1613. Then, it was referring to a person working to carry out calculation, or computation of data. This is why the American Heritage Dictionary (1980) has defined it as *"a person who computes."* And the meaning remained so, until the middle of the 20th century when it was applied as *"a programmable electronic device that can process, store, and retrieve data"* according to the expression of the Webster's Dictionary (1990).

Nevertheless, computers are referred as computing devices, whether or not, they are electronic, programmable, mechanical, or capable of storing and retrieving data. This is why the Techencyclopedia (2003) defines it (computer) as *"a general purpose machine that processes data according to a set of instructions that are stored internally either temporarily or permanently."*

The Encyclopedia Britannica (2003) defines it as *"the contribution of major individuals, machines, and ideas to the development of computing."* This implies that computer is a system, i.e., a group of computer components that work together as a unit to perform a common objective.

Furthermore, let us examining other definitions of computer in the assumed following expressions stated below:

- It is an input-output data processing and storage device or machine
- It is a device that accepts information and manipulates it for some result, based on program or sequence of instructions on how the data is to be processed, and the expected output.
- It is a programmable machine, which can process, store, and retrieve data.
- It is a programmable machine, which receives input, stores and manipulates data, and provides output in a useful format.
- It is an electronic device for storing and analyzing information input into it, for calculating, or controlling machinery automatically.

From the definitions, computer and all equipment attached to it are called *hardware*. The instructions that tell it what to do are called "*software*" or "*a set of programs*". And a program in this concept is a detailed set of humanly prepared instructions that directs the computer to function in specific ways. In addition, referring computer as a programmable machine means that it can execute a programmed list of instructions and respond to new instructions that are given to it.

But, the summary of all these definitions only expressed computer as an electronic device that accept data as input, process the data, and display result as an output. Although, with an alternative functions to store, and to retrieve data depending on the instructions of the user.

Truly, this explanation is not far from the meaning of computer, but, it is of technical functional based, and not generally inclusive. Therefore, we need a general inclusive definition that may be fit for all form of modern computers, and as a result of this, we defined modern computers as *Automatic-Electronic-Data-Processing and Storage Machines* (AEDPSM)*.

*. I was taught with this definition by Instructor Cosmos in the year 1998 at Laro Computer Training Centre, PH, Nigeria.

From this definition of AEDPSM, we expressed computer base on the form of automatic, electronic, data processing, and storage machine, so any machine that possess these properties is computer.

Automatic: Automatic machines are designed to operate themselves in some certain stages of work without any human interfering or control. This certain stage(s) of work(s) depend on the manufacturing built of the machine, as the in-built instruction may be of self-processing of information or self-operating. So, computer as an automatic machine carries out a logical sequence of operations on its own when producing an output, but based on a set of instructions known as program written by the programmer, who owns the running program. This is why most of the computers are called programmable machines.

Electronic: An electronic machine used electrical power and some few small and tiny components referring as chips that help in the controlling and directing of the electrical current movement systematically around the machine. In this matter, computer as an electronic machine also consists of few microchips that boost its operation by controlling and directing the systematic movement of electrical current and other activities in its operations.

Data: The term data (or datums) is a 'plural' of datum. It represents meaningful information, such as personal information, company or any other form of information that are made up of characters or words. By formation, a group of characters will give birth to a word, and group of words when been meaningful will form data. So data machines are machines, which accept data as inputs, process, and display it (the accepted and process data) as output. In this aspect, computer is a data machine that feeds on data in order to execute its operations such as; calculating, analyzing, storing, retrieving, et cetera. For example, the meteorological analysis of weather forecasting by Meteorologists is been carried out in computer through data analysis.

Processing: This is a series of actions performed by the computer itself in order to achieve a targeting task. For instance, by slotting our debit card into an ATM (Automatic Teller Machine) machine, and after entering our command as an input (e.g. password and may be request to do any transaction), the ATM, which is also computer will process the card, therefore, displayed the result on its screen and at the same time pay us (assuming we are to withdraw money) the requested credible amount.

Other examples where we also observed the act of processing are when we check a network service account balance in a mobile phone, which is also computer. For example, when we dialed our *"check balance account code"*, the phone will process our account via the service network and displayed how much credit account residing in our network service account. In addition is the arithmetic logical operation, which we perform daily with our calculator. For example, output displayed on our calculator as a result has been processed by the calculator (which is also computer) before the displayed result.

So, every processing machine is computer, and computer as a processing machine performs the work of storing, locating, analyzing, calculating, sorting, selecting, retrieving of data, making of simple decision of "yes or no", and other processing functions. But, the processing output or result depends on data input made by the user. In addition, every machine that characterized with a processing capability has a processor. The processor however, differs according to their speed rates. A higher processor performs a faster rate of processing than a lower processor, vice-versa.

Storing: A storage machine apart from the default storage is designed to store their information according to the direction of the user. Although, the information to be stored depends on the capacity-storage made of the machines, and type of information the user wants to store. So, computer as a storage machine can store its information in external device, for example, flash, diskette, memory card, and others in one hand, and internal device such as hard disk in the other hand.

Machine: This is any device that uses energy to perform some activities. In a common usage, it is any device that has some parts that perform or assist in some type of work. They required maintenance or servicing and repairing whenever necessary, otherwise it may breakdown as due to lack of maintenance or poor handling. Relatively, computer as a device is like other machines, which used energy and at the same time has components (parts) that perform specific works. It also required maintenance, repairing, and proper handling or it may experience system crash. For this reason, users should handle any available computer with intensive care to avoid a system crash down. It should be repair when necessary and, all the operating guides should be applied.

Generally, the modern answer to our question; what is computer? Is that computer is an Automatic-Electronic-Data-Processing and Storage Machine (AEDPSM). Nevertheless, we may ask about some analog computers like; type-writing machine, analog fuel pump meter machine used in filling stations, and others that are not actually electronic machines. To a certain extent, these machines are also computers. This is because most of them are electromechanical and data processing machines. However, the fact remains that we are now living in a digitalized world and almost all the machines (even some cars) are digitalized, so the uses and inventions of analog computers have paved way (but, not outrightly) to digital computers, therefore our explanation on the meaning of computer is based on the concept of digitalized era.

THE CHARACTERISTICS OF COMPUTER

Like we mentioned early, the first computer were people who struggle for daily computation of data. These people have characters such as speed, storage, accuracy, reliability, processing, communication, consistency, et cetera in carrying out their calculation work as of then. But, due to boredom and human-error in their computation activity in relation to these characters, the invention of computer emerged in order to enhance the works. So our characters of computer are speed, diligence, storage, versatility, accuracy, reliability, processing, communication, precision, consistency, et cetera.

1. **Speed:** Computer works at a high-speed rate, thus much faster than human being. It is invented to work at a high speed in calculating, analyzing and making decisions. For its processing speed, per second is very large time to rate its processing speed as it works on Pico second (a trillion of seconds), and Microsecond (a million of seconds). The time it used to perform an operation, which is processing speed is measured in Hertz such as Kilo Hertz (KHz) for thousands, Mega Hertz (MHz) for millions, and Giga Hertz (GHz) for billions. The higher the Hertz, the higher the processing speed rate.

2. **Storage:** As computer carries out its operation, there is the need for it to store most of the useful programs and data in its internal device such as hard disk, which is an internal storage device of the computer, and external storage devices such as diskette, flash, memory card, et cetera. It has the ability to store information ranging from data such as texts, video, graphic, and sound, et cetera depending on the user.

3. **Diligence:** For work delivering, computer is diligent, as it does not suffer tiredness or lack of concentration like a human being. It performs the last work just like the first work.

4. **Consistency:** Human being can find it difficult in repeating the same pattern of instruction due to boredom and tiredness, but computer can repeat the same instruction repeatedly without losing concentration, therefore, it is consistent.

5. **Versatility:** It can perform different kind of tasks one by one or simultaneously. In one form, depending on the installed software. It can enable the user to do different kind of works at a time. For instance, at one moment a user can be word-processing a document, at next the moment (or on the screen) be playing a game, and also doing other work as it is permitted.

6. **Accuracy:** Not only fast, computer also gives a perfect output depending on input made. It can perform a million operations without error. In addition, it is built in the operational term of "what you see is what you get (WYSIWYG).

7. **Reliability:** It has a very low failure character, which might be trace from old age or improper usage. Despite of this, modern computer can perform very complicated calculations without creating any problem and produces reliable results. In general, computers are very reliable in terms of result-oriented.

8. **Receive-ability:**   Computer is characterized to receive information as data, picture, sound, or voice as input, thus utilize the information for the purpose it is designated for.

9. **Processing:**   Computer can process a given instructions. It can perform different types of processing like addition, subtraction, multiplication, and division. In addition, it also can process information, which require asking of questions and, answering simple questions that involve "yes or no".

10. **Outputting**:   Computer has that character of displaying the output of any information it receives after processing.

11. **Communication**:   Modern PCs have the capability of communicating with other computers. For instance, through a device called Modem (Modulator-Demodulator), computers communicate at distance rate with each other. A Modem is a piece of computer hardware which is used to communicate between distant computers. By modulating, it changes digital data to analog data, as they are transferred from computer to the telephone. In other hand, by demodulating, it changes analog data back to digital data, as they are transferred back from telephone to the computer. In other words, its work is to change the signal from digital, which computers use, to analog, which telephones use, and then back again from analog data to digital data. In addition by means of networking; two or more computers can be connect together to perform the same job specifications. They can share data, instructions, and information together.

THE USES OF COMPUTER

There is that complexity, when it comes to the point of enumerating the uses of computer because the great machine is applicable to all facet works of lives. That is, the uses of computers are available to all human activities. For example, in Developed Countries, even the case of household chores like washing of kitchen utensils are done with computers. Computer can drive a car, do the work of a bodyguard, sells newspaper, and drinks, work as a messenger, work like a police officer, although with some limitations, but do other activities that man can do.

There are the uses of computers in all the industries ranging from extracting, manufacturing, and services industry. The same is to production, which are primary (extracting of raw materials), secondary (the processes of turning the raw materials into finished good) and tertiary (services) production. In addition, these include both works done in educational sector, financial, oil, health, agricultural, administrative sectors, et cetera. The same goes to all form of professions, like Engineering, Social Sciences, Medicine, Pharmacy, Business Management, etc.

Inclusively, there are computer books and programs specialized for economists, engineers, doctors, accountants, administrator, lawyers, teachers, scientists and others. A good example is the use of a Tech-Pack book like App-XL (see www.App-XL.com), which can teach us on how to apply some real world works in Microsoft Excel.

THE LIMITATIONS OF COMPUTER

No matter how great computer may be of its superlative characters, yet, it has some limitations. These limitations include its man-made nature, level of thinking, et cetera.

1. **Man-made:** Computers are a man-made electronic machine. They functions according to the components used in building them. For instance, man may decide to limit their processing speed by reducing the quality of their processors, limiting their accuracy, and as well as defaulting their general characters.

2. **Programming**: The characters of computer are programmed by human being, for instance, their ability to carry out work at a very fast rate is been programmed to do so. In the absent of the programs, they are nothing. So they are made to respond on the instruction given to them by the user.

3. **Thinking**: Although, the concept of artificial intelligence shows that computers can think and take simple decision of "yes or no". But, what they think and make out of their decisions depend on the set of instructions built into they by man. Logically, they cannot think by themselves, expect they are being programmed to do so. Therefore, their thinking process, although been fast and very accurate is linear, so they cannot think randomly like man.

4. **Caring**: Unlike human being, they cannot take care of themselves, so they depend on the user to take care of them.

5. **Judgment**: They cannot make moral judgment over a social issue, unless otherwise they are programmed to respond to such issue. For example, computers cannot judge a criminal case, unless such case is programmed into it.

6. **Creativity:** They are not creative and imaginative, so they cannot create something new, unless it is that particular thing is been programmed into them.

End of Chapter Two of Section-One

Key Terminologies and Meanings

Terminology	Meaning
Batch	A set of programmed command made in a way that a single command can generate the rest of the commands.
Data	It is referring to the plural of datum. For input application, it is a piece of information that can be in the nature of characters, sound, image, or picture.
Diskette	It is an external storage computer device
Hard disk	It is the internal storage device of the computer
Hardware	This is the physical, electronic mechanical components of computer.
Input	A means of supplying information into computer
Output	It is the act of sending result of processed data by the computer.
Processing	It is the act of working on the data or information supply into the computer by the computer in order to produce output.
Program	It is a sequence of instructions written by a developer (programmer) ordering computer on how to perform a specified task. For instance, Programs are developed to tell computers on how to carry out tasks
Software	It is a set of programs designed to make computer be operative and perform tasks.
Terminal	It is a device that enables computer to receive or deliver data.
TES	It means Terminal Emulation Software. It is software that imitates terminal operation.

Objectives Assessment of Chapter Two

1. Examine yourself whether you perfectly achieved the objectives of this last Chapter, if not, read it again. And, if you have any question regarding to what you have learnt, visit **www.onlineworkdata.com**.

2. If you are successful, move to the next Chapter;

"The Classifications of Computer"

Chapter Three of Section-One

The Classifications of Computer

INTRODUCTION

All computers are the same because they all run the same similar logical or operational functions of input-processing-output performances. But, by formation, not all of them are the same because they can be classify by different factors such as physical size, architectural designation, microprocessors, input-signal system, and functions classifications. Therefore, in this chapter, computers are classified base on their physical size, architectural designation, types of microprocessors, input-signal system, and various forms of functions.

BY PHYSICAL SIZE

The physical sizes of computer are classified into mainframe computers, minicomputers, and microcomputers.

Mainframe Computers

Mainframe is computer industry term for a physical large computer. The name comes from the way the machine is been build up, as all its units were hung into a frame, including the main-computer. They are powerful computers used mainly by large organizations for critical applications, typically bulky data processing such as census, industrial and consumer statistics, organizational resource planning, and financial transaction processing.

For pioneering the inventions, many scientists contributed to the inventions of mainframe, but it was not too easy to them, comparing to the case of nowadays that the invention has exploded. For instance, in the early days, in most cases, many mechanisms, or materials still had to be invent before some mainframes were developed. For example, the development of online memory was a crucial phase for the inventions of most of the mainframes, but it was in 1960 when *IBM-7090 console time-sharing* was invented that mainframe uses exploded.

The IBM-7090 Console, 1960

Furthermore, for the construction, in the early days of 1960s, the mainframes output were been displayed via a paper tape, but with time, by an array of burning lamps and when the vacuum tube technology became sophisticated enough to build a monitor, then output as results were now been displayed by means of spots on the screen.

For the Operating system, at first there was no operating system, so most of the mainframes were hard wired. Programming them (the mainframes) meant rewiring panels and setting hundreds of switches to have the machine perform a particular task, such as calculating a table. But, by the time when programming languages like COBOL, ALGOL, and others became available and memory was no longer a problem, thus programmers created operating systems, and inventors do no longer need the technical expert of electrical engineering in order to program computer with an operating system. That made it possible for scientists and other users to quickly make a program and get the results.

History

ENIAC, 1943

Historically, building mainframes started with the ENIAC in 1943, then soon followed by other types such as; Mark-1 (1944), UNIVAC (1952), MIT Whirlwind-1 (1960), including the emerging manufacturers such as Group Bull, DEC, IBM, NEC, Siemens, Unisys, Sun, et cetera. But, because of the development costs only governments and large firms could pay for the development of it.

Moreover, following the development trends, which constitute the traditional and modern types of mainframes; the traditional types were remarkable in the 1960s to have no interactive interface like monitor. They were working with the acceptance of sets of punched cards, paper tape, and magnetic tape and that were operated solely in batch mode in order to support office functions, such as customer billing.

By early 1970s, many mainframes acquired interactive user interfaces and operated as time-sharing computers, supporting hundreds of users simultaneously along with batch processing. It was found that initially, users gained their access through traditional terminals equipped with terminal emulation software, and many of the mainframes supported graphical terminals and, the terminal emulation, until 1980s when graphical user interface became available and the traditional terminals were replaced with PCs in the preference to Web user interface in 1990s. However, this did not indicate the end-use of terminal entirely because most developers and operational staff still use them.

The modern mainframes in the other hand have some improvement, for instance, a modern mainframe is still a very large machine, sometimes tens of square meters. It has usually more than one processor and loads of memory. It often runs between a few mega to several hundred gigabyte (GB) of RAM. It has tons of disk space and other storage facilities in large size and quantities that are not normally found with mini or microcomputers, and can be used by hundreds of users simultaneously.

For marketing, considering the facts[*] obtained when this book was written, from the late 1990's, mainframe manufacturers start to leave the mainframe market, thinking mainframe business to be less profitable, so many of them left the market, therefore leaving IBM as the sole manufacturer. And as the single manufacturer, IBM was able to maintain the market by introducing its product at its own price, and sales goes up as well as profits. Following this, their (IBM) innovations in new mainframe construction set them ahead of others. But, in due time, this was observed by other computer manufacturers like Fujitsu, Hitachi, and NEC, who decided to rejoined the market, therefore made the market more competitive. So since 2002 competition gets stronger again. Although, no matter the tenacity of the competition, as of when this book was written, IBM is still dominates the mainframe computer market, and many of the producers now relying on peripheral productions of it.

*. **Get the facts on IBM vs the Competition- The facts about IBM System z "mainframe."** IBM. *http://www-03.ibm.com/systems/migratetoibm/getthefacts/mainframe.html#4*. Retrieved December 28, 2009

Classification and Characteristics of a Mainframe

There are basic features that classified and characterized mainframe computers, but, the components classifications are as follows:

- a mainframe computer has 1 to 16 CPU's, but modern ones have more;
- its memory ranges from 128MB over 8 Gigabyte on line RAM;
- its processing power ranges from 80 to over 550 million of integers per second;
- it has often different cabinets for storage, RAM, and input/output;
- it is capable of separating processes for task management, program management, job management, serialization, catalogs, inter address space, communication.

Furthermore, associated with the above characteristics of mainframe are other special properties like running in multiple OS, mainly for large computer works, et cetera.

Run in multiple operating systems: Nearly all mainframes have the ability to run (or host) multiple operating systems, and thereby operate not as a single computer, but as a number of virtual machines or computers that execute programs like a physical machine.

Run in multiple machines: Some IBM mainframe computers can run in two (or more) computers in a method that; one in a primary data centre, and the other in a backup data centre. The backup data centre may be established for the reason to checkmate functional or operational failure of the primary data centre mainframe. So it may be fully active, partially active, or on standby. However, this does not dismissed a single running mainframe, but, activities like testing, development, training, and production workload for applications and databases can run on a single mainframe, except for extremely case where the task is too much for the single mainframe to be handled. In practice most people use multiple mainframes linked by Parallel Sysplex (the cluster of IBM mainframes acting together as a single system) and shared DASD (Direct Access Storage Device).

Designed for larger computer works: Among the computing works of a mainframe is designed to handle a very high volume of input and output data processing works. For instance, since the mid-1960s, mainframe designs have included several subsidiary computers (called peripheral processors) which manage the input/output devices, leaving the CPU free to deal only with high-speed memory. So it is common in mainframe computation to deal with massive databases and files such as Giga-record, or Tera-record files. And when compared to a typical PC, mainframes commonly have hundreds to thousands of times of much data storage online, and can access it much faster.

It is cost effective: Cost effectiveness involves the act of comparing costs of different approaches to achieving a given objective. The modern mainframe computer is seen to be cost-effective when compare to its scale of operation. For instance, like any other computing platform, it is dependent on its ability to scale, support mixed workloads, reduce labour costs, deliver uninterrupted service for critical business applications, and several other risk-adjusted cost factors. So the modern mainframe often has unique value and superior cost-effectiveness, especially for large-scale enterprise computations.

Designed for assured integrity on results: For financial transaction computations, mainframes also have execution integrity character to assist user be sure of computed result. For example, System z10 servers effectively execute result-oriented instructions twice, compare results, arbitrate between (or check for) any differences (through instruction of retry and failure isolation), then shift workloads "in flight" to functioning processors, including spares, without any impact to operating systems, applications, or users. The Hewlett-Packard (HP)'s NonStop mainframe is a good example of mainframe with such character.

Minicomputers

The term 'Minicomputer' was coined at the time when most computers were cabinet sized like Mainframe Computers. Minicomputers were much smaller, less powerful, and much less expensive than Mainframes. They usually took up one or a few cabinets' size of a large refrigerator or two, which is unlike a mainframe that would usually filled up a room.

A minicomputer characteristically is designed to support more than one user at a time. It possesses a large storage capacity and operates at a higher speed rate. Like a mainframe, the computer is also used in multi-user system in which various users can work at the same time. It is used in manufacturing processes or handling email that was sent and received by a company. In addition, it is also generally used for processing large volume of data in an organization, and as well used as servers in Local Area Networks (LAN) and Wide Area Network (WAN).

History

The PDP-1 of DEC, 1960

Historically, the Minicomputers evolved in the 1960s in order to describe the 'small' third generation computers that became possible with the use of integrated circuit, and core memory technologies. The first minicomputer was PDP-1 developed in 1960 by DEC. But, the successful minicomputer was the DEC's PDP-8 launched in 1964. The DEC's PDP-8 was known to be at the cost of US$16,000 upwards. But, before its development, there are others like PDP-5, LINC, the TX-0 minicomputers, and others. So the existence of digital equipment gave rise to a number of minicomputer companies such as Massachusetts Route 128, Wang Laboratories, Apollo Computer, Prime Computer, and others.

However, due to some complexities of the machine, then, in 1974 computer called MITS (Micro Instrumentation and Telemetry Systems) Altair 8800 was developed as the first microcomputer by Edward Roberts, Forrest Mims, and others. The MITS Altair 8800 was built with a single-chip microprocessor (known as Intel 8080 CPU) from a microprocessor production company known as *Intel*. So the decline of the minicomputers took place due to the lower production cost of the microprocessor such as Intel 68020, 80286 and the 80386. This therefore, led to the emerging of inexpensive and easily deployable LAN systems, and the desire of the users to be less dependent from the rigid minicomputer manufacturers, and others.

With the passage of time, the period of 1990s brought a change from the uses of minicomputers to inexpensive microcomputers networks. This was accomplished by the development of several versions of operating systems to run on the *Intel x86 microprocessor* designs. In addition, these operating systems have the attribute of server versions that can also support multi-tasking. So microprocessors became more powerful, as CPUs (central processing units) were then built with multiple components.

Furthermore, for the market sharing, the DEC Company was the leading minicomputer manufacturer, at one time the 2nd largest computer company after IBM. But as the minicomputer declined in the face of generic UNIX Corporation servers and Intel Corporation based PCs, not only DEC, but almost every other minicomputer companies including Data General, Prime, Vision, Honeywell and Wang Laboratories, many based in New England also collapsed, and DEC was sold to Compaq in 1998.

Microcomputer

Microcomputer is an antiquated term that refers to computers that used microprocessor in their CPU, rather than vacuum tubes or transistors, which were commonplace before the development of microprocessor. These computers are small enough and can be fit on a desk or operate while holding in a hand. They are the commonest used computers, and very small compare to mainframes and minicomputers. A microcomputer, being a digital computer system that is controlled by a stored program, uses a microprocessor, a programmable read-only memory (ROM), and a random-access memory (RAM). The ROM defines the permanent instructions to be executed by the computer, while the RAM is the functional memory regarded as the primary or temporary data storage of the computer.

Moreover, the computers are built with storage locations, and are capable of handling small, single-business application such as sales analysis, inventory, billing, payroll, administrative works, et cetera. Good examples of them are modern desktop computers, video game consoles, laptops, tablet PCs, and many types of handheld devices, including mobile phones and pocket calculators, as well as industrial embedded systems.

In common usage, a microcomputer is publicly regarded as "personal computer" or 'PC'. This describes it as a single user computer at a time, but can be modified with software or hardware in order to make it serve more than one user. For designation, they are designed to fit well on or under desks or tables, so that they are within easy access of the user. IBM first promoted the term "personal computer" to differentiate themselves from other microcomputers, often called "home computers" as of then. But, unfortunate to IBM, the microcomputer itself was widely imitated, as well as the term by other computer manufacturers. This is because the parts were commonly available to these manufacturers. Nevertheless, the IBM PC was still the dominant and publicly recognized as personal computer, although, this does not cause a derail in the recognition of other microcomputers. Their in-built physical components are mainly *monitor, keyboard* and *system unit* in one hand, and other assisting devices for input and output functions that may be integrated or separated. The system unit constitutes of RAM, ROM, hard disk and others that are usually combined with the CPU, batteries, a power supply unit, printers and some other human interface devices. Although, some of the microcomputers can function with one type of data storage usually RAM, but, for effective and efficient data storage, there is always the need for the secondary data storage, so in the early days external device like cassette deck was used. But, with time, floppy disk and hard disk drives were integrated in the built of some microcomputers, such as desktop, laptop, et cetera.

Types of Microcomputers

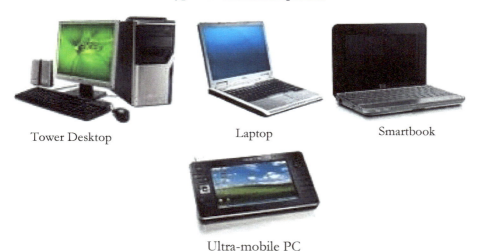

Tower Desktop   Laptop   Smartbook

Ultra-mobile PC

DESKTOPS

The desktop computers are made to be fitted on a desk, and they are normally used at a single location. They exist in a variety of models such as tower orientated (i.e. standing system unit) and horizontal-oriented (i.e. lay-down system unit) models. For compartment, the *tower desktop* involves the separation of the monitor from the system units, and as well as the keyboard. In the other words, the system unit can be tucked behind the monitor. For the horizontally-oriented model, the monitor usually intended to be placed on top of the system unit, in order to save a space on top of the desk, and it is also called *table desktop*.

The operation of a desktop requires powering the *power-on* button of the system unit. During operation, it is usually run on a power supply, which is an external Alternating Current/Direct Current (AC/DC) adapter that supplies power to the computer. Although, to support the computer in event of power failure, most users often connect the power source to Uninterrupted Power Supply (UPS) device, which is an accessories or supportive hardware of computer. It enables computer user to tidy up his/her work at the point when the power supply source of the desktop gets terminated. In addition, desktops also make use of mouse device to support their operations. We will learn more about hardware in chapter two of this Section.

MOBILE COMPUTERS

This comprises laptop, Tablet, Wearable Computers, Calculators, and Personal Digital Assistants (PDAs).

Laptop or Notebook

Unlike desktops are the laptops, which due to their nature of portability can be referred as notebook or notepad computers. A standard laptop is a small mobile computer, typically weighing 3 to 12 pounds (1.4 to 5.4 kg), although older laptops may weigh more. Its screen, keyboard and system units are built together on a portable format of a book. The operation of a laptop requires the opening of it; just the way we open our books, then power it on through the power-on button.

During operation, it is usually run on a single main battery or from an external AC/DC adapter that charges the battery while also supplying power to the computer itself even in the event of a power failure. This very powerful main battery, however, is quite different from the much smaller battery nearly all computers use to run the real-time clock when the computer is out of power supply. To support the in-built keyboard, they may utilize a touchpad (also known as a track pad) or a pointing stick for its operation. In addition, every purchased laptop, being regarded as a notebook has notebook ID (identity). In addition, laptops are also in the built of subnotebook, or smartbook. A subnotebook is a small and lightweight portable computer, with some features of a standard laptop, but smaller in size than the laptop. It is often applied to computers that run full versions of desktop operating systems such as Windows or Linux Operating System, rather than specialized software such as Windows CE or Palm operating system normally found in personal digital assistants.

For size measurability, a standard subnotebook is smaller than a laptop, but larger than handheld computers, i.e., most PDAs and ultra-mobile PCs. It often has smaller-sized screens, usually measuring from 7 inches to 13.3 inches, and a weight from less than 1 kg up to about 2 kg. The savings in size and weight are usually achieved partly by omitting some parts like ports.

Generally, laptops contain components that are similar to their desktop counterparts and perform the same functions, but are miniaturized and optimized for mobile use and efficient power consumption, and also more costly than most desktops.

Personal Digital Assistants (PDAs)

As we mentioned above, another form of microcomputer is Personal Digital Assistant (PDA). PDAs are handheld PCs, known as small or palmtop computers. Their examples are Smartphones (mobile phones), Pocket PCs, PMPs (Portable media players), DAPs (Digital Audio Players), and PDETs (Portable Data Entry Terminals). In designs, most of the new PDAs have both colour screens and audio capabilities, which enable them to be used as mobile phones, web browsers, data entry terminals, or portable media players. Many PDAs can access Internet, intranets, or extranets via Wi-Fi, or Wireless Wide-Area Networks (WWANs). In addition, other good examples of mobile computers are tablet computers such as "ultra-mobile PC" (UMPC), wearable computers like calculators such as scientific type, wrist watch.

History

The history of microcomputers can be trace back in 1968 when Hewlett-Packard Corporation Calculators known as HP 9100B machine was built around and with various levels of programmability, but without microprocessors. Although, subsequent models incrementally added more features. This include the BASIC programming language (e.g. HP 9830A in 1971) and some models that had tape storage and small printers. So following the trends, came the invention of Datapoint 2200 made by Computer Terminal Corporation (CTC) in 1970, Kenbak-1 in 1971, and Sac-State 8008 computer built by a Sacramento State University team led by Bill Pentz in 1972. Furthermore, the introduction of Micral-N in 1973 by a French man called Micral N., which, was the first microprocessor PC sold completely assembled and not as a construction kit.

Though, these microcomputers were for engineering development and hobbyist personal used at this era, and they are sometimes called the "first generation microcomputers". A significant feature is that all of them were essentially boxes with lights and switches. A user had to read and understand binary numbers and machine language to program and use them. Differently, this was not the same to Datapoint 2200, which featured modern designs based on a monitor, keyboard, tape and disk drives.

It was, in 1975 computer called MITS (Micro Instrumentation and Telemetry Systems) Altair 8800 was developed as a better microcomputer than Micral N. The MITS Altair 8800 PC was the first successful commercialized Personal Computer based on a single-chip microprocessor known as SOL-20 from Intel Company. For further improvement of other microcomputers, it was the invention of MITS Altair 8800 that eventually led to the founding and success of many well-known Personal Computer hardware and software companies, such as Microsoft and Apple Computer.

Then, the year 1977 saw the introduction of the second generation microcomputers known as *home computers*, which are better off than the first generation microcomputers. These microcomputers were easier to operate, for example, they have the feature that enable them get connected to a monitor (screen) or TV set, just for visual manipulation of text and numbers. In 1979, there was a launch of the VisiCalc spreadsheet *application software*, which was the first spreadsheet and this turned the microcomputer from a hobby for computer enthusiasts into a business tool. Then, the IBM PC, which was released in 1981 made the term "personal computer" popular.

MITS Altair 8800

BY INPUT-SIGNAL SYSTEM

This form of classification is also referred as *Data Processing Classification*. Generally, computers are also classified base on the way they signalized the information they received as input. The input signal of any computer can be of analog, digital, or hybrid. So for this point, we have analog, digital and hybrid computers.

Analog

An analog (or analogue)computer is a form of computer that uses the continuously-changeable aspects of physical phenomena such as electrical, mechanical, or hydraulic quantities to model computer problem that required solving. In other words, it represents data in continuous form by using physical quantities. Their accuracy depends upon the measurement made, and so not as accurate as the digital computers. These types of computers are used for scientific or engineering purposes. Examples include petrol pump machines, speedometers, and voltammeters.

The analog computers can have a very wide range of complexity, both in work performances and in set up. For example, Slide rulers and nomograms are the simplest, while naval gun fire control computer is among the most complicated. To set-up an analog computer required some conditions like choosing of scale factors with starting values, along with initial condition, creating the required network of interconnections between the computing elements or components, and other essentials.

For sub-classification, the analog computers can be classified into two such as mechanical and electrical analog computer. The mechanical analog computers were very important in gun fire control during the World War II, and the Korean War. They were made in significant numbers.

For practical, most practical mechanical analog computers of any significant complexity used rotating shafts to carry variables from one mechanism to another.

The electronic analog computers typically in their properties have front panels with numerous jacks (single-contact sockets) that permit patch cords (i.e., *flexible wires with plugs at both ends*) to create the interconnections, which defined the problem setup. The computer is built to make use of few to a hundred or more operational amplifiers ("op amps") that performed mathematical operations in the voltage measurement. The op amps, which is used in almost every functional unit (adders, integrators, et cetera) is the basic building block of the electronic analog computer.

Polish Electronic Analog computer, ELWAT

Some operational amplifiers made by Philbrick Researches

Furthermore, the use of electrical properties in analog computers means that calculations are performed normally in real-time, at a speed determined mostly by the frequency response of the op amps and other computing elements. Moreover, it is well known, in particular that the development of transistors made electronic analog computers practical, and before digital computers had developed sufficiently, they (analog computers) were commonly used in science and industry. In addition, the electronic analog computers also have some special high-speed types.

Generally, both mechanical and electrical analog computers have some limitations, whereby no variables can be allowed to exceed the computer's limits. In addition, differentiation was to be avoided, typically by rearranging the 'network' of interconnects, and using integrators in a different sense. However, any physical process, which models a computation, can be interpreted as an analog computer.

Key Components

Analog computers often have a complicated framework, though they have, at their core with a set of key components that perform the calculations, which the operator manipulates through the computer's framework The key components are described as follows:

- The key hydraulic components might include pipes, valves, and containers.
- The key mechanical components might include rotating shafts for carrying data within the computer, miter-gear differentials, etc.
- The key electrical/electronic components might include are precision resistors and capacitors, operational amplifiers, multipliers, et cetera.

The core mathematical operations used in an electric analog computer are summation, integration with respect to time, multiplication, exponentiation, logarithm, and division, although multiplication was more preferable.

History

The history of analog computer cannot leave the Islamic world out, although, the Antikythera mechanism, which was mentioned at the Chapter one is believed to be the earliest known mechanical analog computer. It was discovered in 1901 in the shipwreck, off the Greek Island of Antikythera, between Kythera and Crete, has been dated to be around 100 BC, and was designed to calculate astronomical positions. So, the Islamic world in the 11th century has made record in the invention of most mechanical analog computer including *astrolabe*. As the events included, Medieval Muslim Astronomers produced many different types of astrolabes and used them for over a thousand different problems related to astronomy, astrology, horoscopes, navigation, surveying, timekeeping, prayer, et cetera. For example the Equatorium, which was an astrometic calculating instrument invented by Abū Ishāq Ibrāhīm al-Zarqālī (Arzachel) in Islamic Spain *around* 1015. The castle clock, an astronomical clock invented by Al-Jazari in 1206 has been described by some as the first programmable analog computer. In addition, are the slide ruler, which was invented around 1620 to 1630 as a hand-operated analog computer for doing (at least) simple multiplication and division. Moreover, in 1876, the differential-analyzer, a mechanical analog computer designed to solve differential equations by integration, using wheel-and-disc mechanisms to perform the integration was invented by James Thomson, but got into a limelight within the period of 1920s to 1930s.

Despite, the development of all the above mentioned analog computers, it was in 1897 that Mihailo Petrović, a world-renown Serbian mathematician and inventor, invented one of the first prototypes of analog computers. By 1912 Arthur Pollen had developed an electrically driven mechanical analog computer for fire-control systems, based on the differential-analyzer. The computer was used by the Imperial Russian Navy in World War I. In addition, the paradigm of the differential-analyzer strongly influenced the architecture of the ENIAC, which was indeed designed to replace the differential-analyzer for doing ballistic calculations towards the end of World War II. Then in 1947, the FERMIAC was invented as analog computer by a physicist called Enrico Fermi to aid in his studies of neutron transport. The 1949 made unveil of an invention of MONIAC Computer, which was a hydraulic model of a national economy. In 1960, Newmark analogue computer was invented. The computer was made up of five units. It was used to solve differential equations and is currently housed at the Cambridge Museum of Technology in UK as of when this book was written.

Newmark Analog, 1960

A Reconstructed Antikythera

Polish Analog Computer known as AKAT-1

Digital Computers

A digital computer is a programmable device that processes information by manipulating symbols according to logical rules. It runs data in terms of digits and proceeds in discrete steps from one state to the next. In this aspect, even symbols like numbers, alphabets, sounds, and images are represented digitally.

Unlike analog computers, digital computers can only approximate a range by assigning large numbers of digits to a state description and by proceeding in randomly small steps, therefore, been termed 'digital' in order to distinguish it from that of the analog computer. Although, it manipulates symbols, not actually digits, despite the name, while analog computers manipulate electronic signals or other physical phenomena that act as models. So, today the word 'computer' has come to be effectively synonymous with "digital computer", due to the existence of very few of analog computations.

In functional processes, a digital computer will convert all input data into binary form, process them in the format of the binary form, then displayed the processed information in discrete values. In this manner, the processed information is converted back to binary form in order to have accuracy in any of its data computation.

The computer (i.e. digital computer) is in existing of different kinds, ranging from embedded systems (dedicated computers), desktop computers, minicomputers, mainframe computers, PDAs, and the supercomputers. Presently, they are the most formed uses of computers in the world. That is why, all the institutions in the world such as governments, international communities, profit and non-profit organizations are on the trend of using it.

History

Historically, the story of digital computer cannot do without the remembrance of George Stibitz, who is internationally recognized as the father of modern digital computer. In 1937, Stibitz developed the first digital computer, therefore, gained the international recognition as the father of the modern digital computer. In November 1937, while working with Bell Labs, Stibitz invented and built a relay-based calculator, which was the first computer to use binary circuits to perform an arithmetic operation. Although, with subsequent of time, computers developed after Stibitz computer were featured with greater sophistication including with complex arithmetic and programmability. However, before Stibitz computer, the need to develop digital computers got significant in the Second World War, and at this period, there was the need for computers to feature greater programmability and higher speed as in replacement of the previous computers. So this need was met in the inventions of computers like Colossus (1943), Mark-1 (1944), ENIAC (1946), UNIVAC (1952), EDVAC (1953), IBM 709 in 1959, etc.

Stibitz Computer, 1937

Hybrid Computers

They are computers built with some features of analog computers and that of digital computers. In other words, a hybrid computer is built with the combination of the best features of analogue and digital computers. In functional processing, most hybrid computers accept analogue inputs and displayed digital output values, i.e. after processing. The hybrid computers are used in highly scientific environments. They have the speed of the analogue and the accuracy of the digital computer. The digital component normally serves as the controller and provides logical operations, while the analog component normally serves as a solver of differential equations. A good example of hybrid computer is MSI notebook.

Though, we may ask why developing hybrid computers? Generally, analog computers are extraordinarily fast, and can solve most complex equations at the rate of a fractional speed of light. But, its precision (repeatability) is not good. They are limited to three, or at most, four digits of precision. But, digital computers, although, been quite slow when compared to analog computers, can be develop in a mode of action where it can be taking solution of equations to the point of unlimited precision. For example, the speed of a digital computer for a calculation may be slow to be of much use when compare to that of analog computer for weather calculations, but, it precision may be better compare to that of the analog computer, which is prone to insufficiency. In addition, recent upsurge in the use of physiologic data for medical diagnostic and treatment procedures have prompted the medical profession in the use of computer to automate and reduce the time required for data processing, and digital computer has traditionally been used to perform these tasks. However, a hybrid computer has been found to provide many advantages over the digital computer, especially where online data processing is a main task.

A Hybrid Notebook Computer

BY ARCHTECTURAL DESIGNATION

Computers can be classified base on human accessibility and interferences. Some computers in order to prevent third parties interference or protect privacy are built with some installation in order to restrict access, while some are built with *interoperability* for unrestricted access. With unrestricted access, human interference is freely permitted. The unrestricted access computers are termed as *"open systems"* and that of the restricted access are *"close systems"*.

In this aspect, interoperability is a property referring to the ability of diverse systems and organizations to work together in the production and uses of a particular system.

Opened-System and Closed-System

Opened-system is referred as system that interacts with other systems or the outside environment. It is computer design system with uniform industry standards, compatible with any similar type of system or part. In other words, it is a system that provides some combination of interoperability, portability, and *opened software standards*. In this manner, it has specific installations that are configured to allow unrestricted access to people and/or other computers, just for networking, and product enhancement, so open free access both to the third-party and second-party. For such installations, third-party is allowed to develop software and hardware for the interoperability of the system, and as well enhance the productive of the system.

The possibility of an Opened-system exists as a manufacturer gives accessibility to its products via the product open source (*software's source code and rights regarding their redistributions.*). For example, the Windows Personal Computer is an opened-system, although the fundamental standards are controlled by Microsoft, Intel, and AMD (Advanced Micro Devices) Incorporate. But, thousands of the hardware devices such as mouse, printers, keyboards, speaker, and others, including software applications are created and sold by other vendors for the Windows Personal Computer usage. This is why various components of different vendors (i.e., producers and sellers) can be found in a single system. And not only been together, they also function together. In addition, the Linux operating system is another good example because it allows the uses of so many types of computer hardware and software in its usage than any other operating system.

In a reverse manner, closed-system is a system in which some specifications are kept secret to prevent interference from third-party and/or second-party. In other words, it is a system, which has relatively little interaction with other systems, as the vendor or manufacturer place restriction from third-party and/or second-party modifications or providing supportive software and hardware over the system. That is to say, closed-system is known to be featured with third-party restriction. The system is bound to restrict third-party software installation, third-party hardware from interoperating with them, and third-party enhancement from improving the product.

The table below shows some good examples of closed and opened system.

Program Software	Closed-system	Opened-system
Antivirus	Norton	AVG
Operating System	Microsoft Windows	Linux
Web browser	Internet Explorer	Firefox or Mozilla

Historical Cases

The movement of free and open source software was launched in 1983, although before the incidence, earlier software users indirectly or directly via practical or social reason has campaign for such. The movement was launched by Richard Stallman as a reaction to the growing trend of developers blocking these freedoms by only publishing the runnable version of the software and not the modifiable source code. The movement which was known as "The free software movement" was launched in order to give right to software users to freely study, modify and redistribute software.

However, in the existence of the pro-launching, and post-launching of the movement, there are some incidents, which took place in the software and hardware industry, for example, the historical issue of Linux, UNIX, IBM, and Microsoft.*

Linux and UNIX

In 1980s, many people liked to use an Operating System (OS) called UNIX, but, due to the fact that it restricted users from sharing and improving the system, some people made a new operating system that would work like it (UNIX), and a feature that permits anybody to share or improve it. This particular operating system was called **MINIX** (formed from **MI**NIMAL and U**NIX**). It is a UNIX-like computer operating system based on a Microkernel Architecture.

In developing MINX, Andrew S. Tanenbaum wrote it so that it could serve as a teaching tool for university students that want to learn how operating systems worked. With time, a group of people called the **GNU** (**G**NU's **N**ot **U**nix) Project Team wrote different parts of a new operating system called GNU. But, the operating system did not have all the parts in order to function like UNIX.

Then in 1991 Linus Torvalds began to work an OS that will replacement MINIX, and be free for use, and as well cost nothing. Linus started the project when he was attending the University of Helsinki. This eventually became the Linux kernel. He wants to Internet and shared the Linux kernel, which he developed with some groups of MINIX users. By this experiment, he changed his source code from MINX to the opened-system of GNU, which became better to his project.

The GNU General Public License (GPL) in its existence is a software license that lets people change any part of the code they want to, as long as they share any changes they make with the people they give their software to. The software from GNU was all licensed under the GNU General Public License, so that Linus and the other people who developed the Linux operating system make used of it. For example, to make the Linux kernel suitable for use with the code from the GNU Project, Linus Torvalds started a switch from his original license (which did not allow people to sell it) to the GNU GPL. At this time, Linux and GNU developers worked together by integrating GNU code with Linux, therefore made Linux a free operating system. So because of the way that the new operating system was created by combining the work of the GNU project and Linus Torvalds, many people say that it is better to use the name GNU/Linux, but most people just say "Linux". Since then, thousands of programmers and companies have worked to make Linux better since it is an open system.

*. http://en.m.wikipedia.org/wiki/History_of_free_and_open-source_software

The Role of UNIX in Open System

Historically, the opened-system was popularized in the early 1980s. It was mainly to describe systems based on UNIX product, especially in dissimilarity to the more invented mainframes and minicomputers that were in used at that time. Unlike older legacy systems (or patent rights), the newer generation of UNIX systems featured standardized programming interfaces and peripheral interconnects in their products in order to encourage third party development of hardware and software relative to those products.

Although before this time, there was a dispute between some companies like Amdahl and Hitachi going to court to secure right that will enable them sell their systems and peripherals, which were compatible with IBM's mainframes, so by the legacy of open system, the matter was brought to an end. Then, in the 20th century, the open systems concept was duly promoted by UNIX vendors who were significant promoters, despite that IBM and other companies resisted the trend of the promotion for decades. But as of this period, the system became more formalized with the emergence of independently administered software standards such as the Open Group's Single UNIX Specification.

Today, due to the fact that computer users are using high degree of both hardware and software interoperability, so in the first part of the 21st century many of these same legacy system vendors, particularly IBM, Hewlett-Packard, and Sun Microsystems adopted in the application of open systems, which is now general.[1]

The Role of Microsoft Corporation

In 2006 Microsoft launched its CodePlex open source code hosting site. This was done in order to provide hosting for open source developers who are targeting Microsoft platforms. To encourage people more, in July 2009, they open-sourced some *Hyper-V*-supporting patches for the Linux kernel, because they were required to do so by the GNU GPL and contributed to the mainline kernel. In addition, Microsoft's *F# compiler*, created in 2002 was also been released as open-source under the Apache license. The F# compiler as a commercial product was incorporated into Visual Studio, which is not that an open-source. In the other hand, Hyper-V, which is codenamed *Viridian* and formerly known as Windows Server Virtualization is a native *hypervisor* that enables platform virtualization on x86-64 systems.[2]

1. http://en.m.wikipedia.org/wiki/open_system_(computing)
2. http://en.m.wikipedia.org/wiki/History_of_free_and_open-source_software

BY ELECTRONIC SIGNAL SWITCH

Classifying computers by electronic signal, we are referring the generational development of computers with periodical devices used to switch, modify, or create an electrical signal by controlling the movement of electrons in a low-pressure space.

The earlier computers were using electromechanical relay device, and then later came the development of vacuum tube, transistor, and integrated circuits devices.

Electromechanical Relay Computers

Relay computers are computers that used electromechanical relay. In this manner, a relay is an electrically operated switch used by electromechanical computers to switch, modify or create electronic signal. They were extensive used in telephone exchange and early computers to perform logical operations. To other appliances, they work according to the designated purposes. For instance, many relays used an electromagnet to operate a switching mechanism, although other operating principles are also used.

How they work, relays function in finding applications where it is necessary to control a circuit by a low-power signal, or where several circuits must be controlled by one signal. It can be used in long distance telegraphic circuits, repeating the signal coming in from one circuit, and re-transmitting it to another. Examples of computers with electromechanical relays are Z4 built by Konrad Zuse in late 1930s, Mark-1 developed in 1944 by Prof. Howard Aiken, a lecturer in Harvard University, George Stibitz computer of 1937, and Atanasoff–Berry Computer (ABC) of 1942.

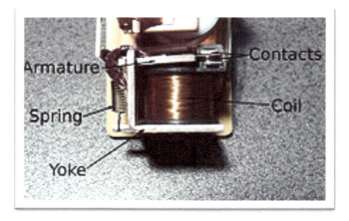

Simple electromechanical relay

Vacuum tube Computers

Vacuum computers are computers, which are using vacuum tubes. In electronic appliances, a vacuum tube referring as electron tube or thermionic valve is a device used to amplify, switch, otherwise modify, or create an electrical signal by controlling the movement of electrons in a low-pressure space This form of computers were critical to the development of electronic technology, which drove the expansion and commercialization of radio broadcasting, television, radar, sound reproduction, large telephone networks, analog and digital computers, including industrial process control. Though, some of these applications are pre-dated electronics, but it was the vacuum tube that made them widespread and practical in uses.

For development, though, there was the need to meet the reliability demand, required by the early computers due to the failure of the relay functions. This facilitated the need to build special *"computer vacuum tubes"* with extended cathode life. The tubes were heavily used in the early generations of electronic devices, such as radios, televisions, and first generation computers such as the Colossus, which used 2000 vacuum tubes, the ENIAC which used nearly 18,000 vacuum tubes, the IBM 709 and others.

However, this first generation of electronic computers that were using vacuum tubes failed because the tubes were generating large amounts of heat, and as well bulky and unreliable. So within the late 1950 to 1960, these reasons of the failure of vacuum tubes led the invention of the second generation of computers, which featured boards filled with individual transistors and magnetic memory core, therefore brought the emergency of transistor computers.

IBM Vacuum Tubes from 1950s computers

Transistor Computers

The transistor computers are the computers that used transistor instead of vacuum tube. A transistor is a semiconductor device used to amplify and switch electronic signals. It is made of a solid piece of semiconductor material, with at least three terminals for connection to an external circuit of a device.

For a simple operation, the essential usefulness of a transistor comes from its capability to use a small signal applied between one pair of its terminals to control a much larger signal at another pair of terminals. In regard, it can control its output in proportion to the input signal, that is, it can act as an amplifier in one hand, or can be used to turn current on/off in a circuit as an electrically controlled switch, where the amount of current is determined by other circuit elements. In addition, one good advantage of transistor computers is longevity as some transistorised devices including computers can stay up to 30 years.

For computer development, Metrovic 950, IBM 1401, IBM 7080, and Harwell CADET of 1955 are good examples of transistor computers. But, in the quest to develop computer with a higher processing speed, the device called integrated circuit (IC) were then included in the development of computers, so we have IC computers.

Assorted Discrete Transistors

Integrated Circuit Computers

The IC also known as microcircuit, microchip, silicon chip, chip or microprocessor in advance is a single physical component that constitutes several transistors, which brought the innovation of integrated circuit computers. The first ICs were based on Small-Scale Integration (SSI) circuits, which had around 10 devices per circuit (or 'chip'), followed by the use of Medium-Scale Integrated (MSI) circuits, which had up to 100 devices per chip, and the development of the Large-Scale Integration (LSI) with 1000 devices per chip, and Very Large-Scale Integration (VLSI) with 100,000 devices per chip.

For classification, ICs can be classified into analog, digital, and hybrid chip. The Digital Chip can contain anything from one to millions of FLOPs (floating point operations per second), and other circuits in a few square millimeters. They allow high speed, low power dissipation, and reduced manufacturing cost compared with board-level integration. These digital ICs, typically microprocessors, and microcontrollers work using binary mathematics to process "one and zero" signals. This is unlike the Analog Chip such as sensors, power management circuits, and operational amplifiers, which works by processing continuous signals. They perform functions like amplification, active filtering, demodulation, mixing, et cetera. Furthermore, the Hybrid Chip is another form of the chip that combined analog and digital circuit located on a single chip in order to create functions such as analog-digital converter, and digital-analog converter. For instance, the hybrid IC can be found in communication enhance device like MODEM.

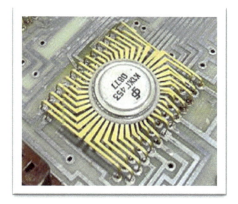

Early USSR made IC

Generally, for comparison, there are two main advantages of IC computers over transistor, and vacuum computers. These advantages are in costing and performances. The production cost of an IC is low because the chips, with all their components, are printed as a unit by photolithography, and not constructed as one transistor at a time. In addition, much less material is used to construct a circuit if a packaged IC dies. This is not the same in vacuum and transistor.

For performances, IC computers performances are higher since the components can switch quickly and consume little power when compared to the transistor computers. This is because the components are small and close together. For instance, as of the year 2006, chip areas range from a few square millimeters to around 350 mm², with up to 1 million transistors per mm². Though, examples of IC computers can be range from the second generation computers to these days' present computers, including almost all the electronic equipment we are using today.

BY MICROPROCESSOR

The microprocessor (known as advanced integrated circuits) is the component of the personal computer that do the actual processing of data. A microprocessor is a CPU that fits on one microchip or integrated circuit. It incorporates most or all of the functions of a CPU on a single integrated circuit. For classification, computers can be classified base on microprocessor differences. This is because different computers came with different microprocessors, but, due to the existing numerous microprocessors, we only mention most of them used by some computers.

As of when this book was written, the most commonly used microprocessors in PCs are made by Intel, which emanated from the period IBM chose the Intel 8088 chip for the original IBM PCs, since then, most PCs clones have used one of the below Intel series of CPUs.

- 8088 - used in IBM PC
- 80286 - used in IBM PC
- 80386 - used in first PC clone from Compaq
- 80486 – use in 486 PC
- Pentium
- Pentium II
- Pentium III – by most computers
- Pentium 4 - Most desktop PCs in 2004 used the P4 chip.
- Pentium M – Also use by most desktop, since 2007
- Celeron 266, Celeron 300, Celeron 1500, et cetera
- Intel Pentium Dual-Core,
- Quad-Core Processor
- Multi-Core Processor, and
- Others that are not mentioned.

Note that most of these 'processors' will be treated in Chapter two.

BY UNIQUE FUNCTIONS

Computer can also be classified base on unique functions, such as supercomputing, servers, workstations, portable data entry terminals, embedded systems, grid computing, and quantum computing.

Supercomputing

Computers who perform supercomputing are called supercomputers. A Supercomputer is not a mainframe computer as many people may have thought. They are the biggest and fastest machines today, which are used when billion or even trillions of calculations are required. They have the highest computing power or high processing speed compared to other computers. For example, it will take a single personal computer more than few days (or weeks) to calculate a weather map, which will result from the predictions of the weather from several days old when the map is finished. But, a supercomputer does the same job in few minutes. This is because of its multiprocessing technique. For instance, one supercomputer can be built with the interconnecting of hundreds of microprocessors.

People who use supercomputer are mostly scientists performing mass computing at ultra-high speed. They use such computers in all imaginable disciplines, such as space exploration and related imagery, earthquake prediction, physics studies, gene technology, industrial and technological applications, creating simulations for building airplanes, creating new chemical substances, new materials, and testing car crashes without having to crash a car. In addition, they are mainly used where it will take more than few days to get the results or when the results are impossible for a slower computer to calculate.

For construction and costing, the construction of any supercomputer is a tremendous task, and the cost is a very expensive one. To produce a single supercomputer from the laboratory to the market may involve several years. Its production can exhaust an entire resource of an organisation. This is why these days, the production of any of it (supercomputer) may require government financial support. In addition, organizations, government, or agencies who hired supercomputers for usage are charge according to the time they use the computer for the works.

History

Historically, before 1965, there were some experimental-supercomputers, such as Atanasoff-Berry Computer (1939), Konrad Zuse -Z2 (1940), ENIAC (1942), etc. They were fast, but not fast enough. So following the trend of engineering and science invention era of that period, industry and government organizations primarily in USA felt the urgent need for faster and mass computing computers. This is because, the processes of calculating a simple stress module for designing engines were taken several days on a contemporary mainframe, and was exhausting all available resources. Then, this rise the need for a search of a new class of computing, which can enhance faster calculation. It was in this period that the first successful supercomputer known as CDC 6600 was invented in 1964 by Seymour Cray, i.e. Cray Inc.

The CDC 6600 is built with speed of 9 Megaflops (i.e. 9 million floating operation, per second). The FLOPs are mostly addition, subtraction, and multiplication with enough digits of precision to model and run continuous phenomena such as weather forecasting, earthquake prediction, et cetera

Following time, then, other supercomputers were IBM 1360 (1966), Texas Instruments; Advanced Scientific Computer (ASC) of 1967, UNIVAC 9400 (1968), Seymour Cray CDC 7600 with 40 Megaflops (1969), UNIX (1970), CRAY-1 (1976), DEC's VAX11-780 of 1978, and Cray X-MP (1982). In addition, the year 1984 created a new generation of supercomputers, and then emerged the development of parallel processing supercomputers. At this time, the mainstream supercomputers were S-810/20 made by Hitachi, FACOM VP 200 by Fujitsu, SX-2 by NEC and C-1 by Convex.

Then in the year 1986, there emerged IBM 3090 VPF, CRAY Y-MP (1989), and ASCI Red (1997), which was the first *teraflop* (trillion floating operations, per second) computer. The year 2000 brought the IBM Blue Gene development, which was the first *special purpose supercomputer* and was used for modeling human proteins in order to be able in separating human genetic code, which can help pharmaceutical laboratories to develop medicines. The least, not the last is in 2002; NEC's Earth Simulator that can run at 35.61 teraflops. It consists of 640 supercomputers and, it is primarily designed for environmental simulations. Although been stated early, below is the first successful supercomputer (CDC 6600), which was invented in 1964 by Seymour Cray, i.e. Cray Incorporate.

CDC 6600 of Cray

Supercomputers versus Mainframe computers

The distinction between supercomputers and mainframes computers can be difficult to outlines, despite of this, in our attempt, supercomputers tend to be custom built and focus on processing power to do one task. Mainframes, while providing a lot of processing power, focus more on data input, and generally perform many data handling operations that involve minor computations.

Supercomputers have capabilities far beyond mainframe computers. For instance, their speed ranges from 100 million-instruction-per-second to well over three billion. In addition, because of their sizes, they sacrifice a certain amount of flexibility, are therefore not ideal for providing a variety of user services. However, in order to handle minor programs or perform slower speed computation, or smaller volume operation, they need the assistance of mini-computers that will serve as front-end processor. The below table displayed the difference between supercomputers and mainframe computers

Differences	
Mainframe Computer	**Supercomputer**
Slower in speed than Supercomputers	The biggest machines today, and as faster in speed than Mainframes
Build for variety of tasks.	Often purpose-built for one or a very few specific institutional tasks, e.g. simulation and modeling
Generally focus on problems, which are limited by input/output and reliability including solving multiple business problems such as banking, airline services, et cetera.	Generally focus on problems which are limited by calculation of speed, for example, nuclear weapon speed computation.
Designed for simple computations that involve huge amounts of external data. For example, insurance business or payroll processing applications that are mostly used by government agencies, business firms, and Schools.	Designed for complicated computations, which often take place largely in memory. For example, weather forecasting, and nuclear weapon development.
It tends to have numerous support-service processors, which assist the main CPU tasks.	It is designed with no much service processors.
Examples of Mainframes are IBM 7090 console time-sharing, Mark-I, ENIAC, and Whirlwind.	Examples of Supercomputers are CDC 6600, CRAY2, NEC SX-3, CRAY XMP, and PARAM.
It is use as controlling nodes in Wide Area Networks (WAN), which is a system where it will serve as server systems and many smaller computers can be connected to it in order to form a communication network. Although, the connected local computers work with their own processors.	It is built with a host processor for other local computers and timesharing networks. Although, the connected local computers work on the host processor of the supercomputer.
They are measured in millions of integer operations per second (MIPS), Examples of integer operations include adjusting inventory counts, matching names, indexing tables of data, and making routine yes or no decisions.	They are measured in floating point operations per second (FLOPs). Floating point operations are mostly addition, subtraction, and multiplication with enough digits of precision to model continuous phenomena such as weather.

Server Computing

This is a computing system runs by a server computer, which is known as enterprise server. It is computer system that provides essential services across a network, to private users inside a large organization or to public users in the internet. For instance, in most cases, a particular computer for example, mainframe, which is generally made to handle a variety of tasks, can be converted to work as a server computer. In this form of function, the actual data to be process by the mainframe will be assigned to other PCs in the means of networking. For example, while the mainframe works for storing of the data, the PCs will be processing the data. But, many smaller servers are actually PCs that have been dedicated to the task of storing data for other PCs. In other instances, many small computers (essentially specialized PCs) are designed to work in concert as a single server. Examples are database server, file server, and web server.

By server functions, a *"Database server"* is a large computer dedicated for database management system (DMBS). In this aspect, such computer manages the collection of computer database work. In the other way, it is computer program that provides database services to other computer programs or computers, based on the definition of the client–server model.

A "*File server*" manages a large collection of computer files in network. In a broad way, it is computer attached to a network that has the primary purpose of providing a location for shared disk access, i.e. shared storage of computer files (such as documents, sound files, photographs, movies, images, databases, etc.), which can be accessed by the workstations that are attached to the computer network. Moreover, in this computation, the server highlights the role of the computer in the client–server scheme, where the *clients* are the workstations using the storage. In addition, the file server is usually not performing any calculations, and does not run any programs on behalf of the clients, rather it is designed primarily to enable the rapid storage and retrieval of data where the heavy computation is provided by the workstations.

The "*Web server*" processes web pages and web applications. For instance, with a web server, the processing of website pages and application on internet browsing become available. This computation is possible via the use of Hypertext Transfer Protocol (HTTP), over the World Wide Web (www).

Workstation Computing

A workstation is a high-end microcomputer designed for technical or scientific applications. It can also be refer as a mainframe computer terminal or a PC connected to a network for scientific or technical applications. They are primarily fixed to be used by one person at a time, commonly connected to a Local Area Network (LAN) and run multi-user operating systems. Though, among the functional principles of workstation are high performance of CPUs, hardware support for floating-point operations, large memory configurations, high-speed networking, high-performances of 3D graphics hardware, high capacity data storage, extremely reliable components, tight integration between the operating system and the hardware, et cetera.

History

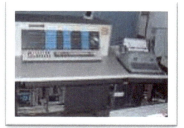

IBM 1620

The first computer that might qualify as a 'workstation' was the IBM-1620, a small scientific computer designed to be used interactively by a single person sitting at the console. It was introduced in 1959. One peculiar feature of the machine was that it lacked any actual arithmetic circuitry. To perform addition, it required a memory-resident table of decimal addition rules. This saved cost for the users, therefore make IBM to make it inexpensive. The machine was code-named CADET, which some people waggishly claimed meant "*Can't Add, Doesn't Even Try*". Nonetheless, it rented initially for $1000 a month. Then in 1965, IBM introduced the IBM 1130 scientific computer, which was meant as the successor to the IBM-1620. Although, prior to the IBM-1620 and others, the early examples of workstations were generally dedicated minicomputers, and any system designed to support a number of users would instead be reserved exclusively for one person. A notable example was the PDP-8 from DEC, regarded to be the first commercial minicomputer. Another is the Lisp machines developed at Massachusetts Institute of Technology (MIT) in the early 1970s, which pioneered some of the principles of the workstation computer, as they have high-performances, networked, single-user systems intended for heavily interactive use.

In the early 1980s, a high-end workstation had to meet the "3M computer" standard. The "3Ms" are memory with a megabyte capacity, a Megapixel display (roughly 1000x1000), and at least a Mega-FLOPs (Million FLOPs) compute performance. Today, workstations had offered higher performance than personal computers, especially with respect to CPU and graphics, memory capacity, and multitasking capability. They are optimized for the visualization and manipulation of different types of complex data such as 3D mechanical design, engineering simulation (such as computational fluid dynamics), animation, and rendering of images, and mathematical plots. Take for instance, consoles consist of a high-resolution display, a keyboard, and a mouse at a minimum, but also offer multiple displays, graphics tablets, and 3D mice (devices for manipulating and navigating 3D objects and scenes). In addition, for timely engineering, medical, and graphics production tasks, the workstation is hard to beat. Although, it tended to be very expensive, typically several times than the cost of a standard PC. For example, most manufacturers of workstation computers are Acer, Alienware, Apple Inc., AVADirect, and BOXX Technologies.

Portable Data Entry Terminals

Terminals are devices that enable computers to receive or deliver data. Computer terminals are greatly depending on the format of the data they handled. For example, a simple early terminal comprised a typewriter keyboard for input and a typewriter-printing element for alpha-numeric output. A more recent variation includes the keyboard for input and a television-like-screen to display the output. Contrarily, a terminal computing is associated with decentralized computing. This signifies that most computing takes place somewhere else than where the terminal is physically situated.

For the process of computation, Portable Data Entry Terminals (PDET's) are handheld devices, which are used for the recording and capturing of data away from the computers that they are linked to them.

On how they functions, most of these handheld devices use light source to read special characters and convert them into electrical signals to be sent to the CPU of the computer. They can be of machine-reading characters made of magnetized particles. For instance, in the case of barcode, they are photoelectric devices that read codes by means of reflected light. They can serve as data collecting devices, which may be located in a warehouse or factory or wherever the activity that is generating the data is located. They are used for image processes and as well other terminal activities. Other examples of PDETs include Barcode readers, Optical Mark Readers (OMR), Optical Character Recognition (OCR), Scanner, Magnetic-Ink Character Recognition (MICR), and Magnetic Stripe Reader (MSR).

Embedded Systems

Embedded systems can be compared to "computers on ICs or dedicated computers." They are general purpose CPUs, which is a part of a machine or device. They run a program that is stored in read only memory (ROM), and are only intended to operate on a specific machine or device. In the other way, they are self-contained pre-programmed computing devices built on IC board, which mostly have no connections outside the environment where that particular type of computing takes (physically) place. They are found in every machine that performs self-regulating, self-controlling, and self-checking operations. Most of the machines are microcontrollers designed embedded applications, therefore regarded as embedded systems.

Practically all consumer electronics, automobiles, and industrial machines are designed for embedded applications today. They are intended to operate within themselves. For example, a DVD player machine when playing performs self-regulating, self-controlling, and self-checking operations, a remote control for consumable electronics, and others, which can operate self-automatic operations under embedded designations with microcontrollers, therefore, regarded as embedded systems.

Furthermore, embedded systems are typically required to operate continuously without being reset or rebooted (to re-on in case of malfunctioning), and once employed in their task the software usually cannot be modified. For instance, an automobile may contain a number of embedded systems; however, a washing machine and a DVD player would contain only one. The CPUs used are slower and less expensive than those found in Personal Computers, but, generally they only have to conduct a single function.

Microcontrollers

As we mentioned above, "most of the machines are microcontrollers designed embedded applications, therefore regarded as embedded systems". Nevertheless, a microcontroller in its development is a small computer on a single integrated circuit containing a processor, memory, and programmable input/output (I/O) peripherals. Like mentioned, they are designed for embedded applications, which is in contrast to the microprocessors used in PCs or other general purpose applications.

As a single IC , a microcontroller may has features like CPU, I/O serial ports, peripherals like timers, event counters, ROM, RAM, Flash memory, A/D (analog-to-digital) converters, Controller Area Network (CAN) for system interconnectivity, and other features not mentioned.

In comparison, both embedded systems and microcontrollers are synonymously in used, but, while embedded systems described devices that are in embedded designation with microcontrollers, and then microcontrollers exist as computers designed for embedded applications, i.e. computers made for the development of embedded systems. Some electronic devices with embedded designations of microcontrollers are regarded as embedded systems. Most of these devices are automobile engine control systems, consumer electronics, implantable medical devices, remote controls, office machines, power-on tools, electronic toys, et cetera. In addition, microcontrollers usually have no keyboard, screen, disks, printers, or other recognizable I/O devices of a PC, and may lack human direct (physical) interaction devices of any kind.

Furthermore, a DVD player machine for example, is an embedded system built with a microcontroller, which enables the machine to carry out its activities suchlike self-regulating, self-controlling, and self-checking operations. The microcontroller in the machine is on a single IC board; it contained a processor, memory, and programmable input/output peripherals (not like that of PCs), and has no keyboard, screen, hard disk or printing port.

PIC 13F8720 Microcontroller

Grid Computing

Grid computing is not popular in Information, Communication and Technology (ICT). By grid computing, we are referring to computing done by multiple number of the same class of computers clustered together for such computing purposes. So a grid computer is nothing else than a multiple number of the same class of computers clustered together for the computation of specific operations. As the case often, the term clustering is a term for "network connecting technology".

Practically, to establish a grid computer, the clustered multiple computers, which will be at same class, will be connected through a super-fast network, they will share a single system unit with the inclusive devices such as hard disk drives, printers, mass memory, including a sophisticated operating system that will take care of the load sharing during computing and processing.

One peculiar character of grid computing is that the more number of the clustered computers, the higher the computing power of the central controlling computer, therefore, causing it to grow into a supercomputer depending on the size of the clustering. In addition, comparing it (grid computer) to the mainframe and supercomputer, the grid computer is mostly build from a large number of self-contained computers. At least the separated machines or computers could work-stand-alone in any computation, and as well work individually on their own. Mostly with grid computing, organizations can optimize computing and data resources, pool them for large capacity workloads, share them across networks, and enable collaboration. In addition, grid computing also enables the actualization of an effective computing system and data resources distribution such as processing, network bandwidth, and storage capacity to create a single system image, granting users and applications seamless access to large ICT capabilities.

In comparison, like website users' application, where an internet user views a unified instance of content of pages through the Website, a grid user essentially sees a single, large virtual computer. In addition, the computing keeps complexity hidden, therefore, make multiple users to enjoy a single and unified experience. Although, unlike the website users' application that mainly enables communication, grid computing enables full collaboration toward common business goals. But, like peer-to-peer (user-to-user) system, grid computing allows users to share files. But, unlike peer-to-peer, it allows many-to-many sharing, in most case; not only files but other resources as well.

Generally, grid computing can be seen as the latest and most complete evolution of more familiar ICT development in the area of cluster and distributive computing.

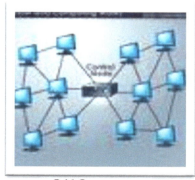

Grid Computer

Parallel Computing

Parallel Computing (also called parallel processing) is the ability of computer to carry out multiple operations or tasks simultaneously. In other words, it is the simultaneous use of more than one CPU or processor core to execute a program, which is a system of multiple computational threads.

Ideally, parallel processing makes programs run faster because there are more CPUs or cores running the computation. In practice, it is often difficult to divide a program in such a way that separate CPUs or cores can execute different portions without interfering with each other. Most computers have just one CPU, but some models have several, and multi-processors, which is now becoming the norm. For instance, with a single-CPU or single-core computers, it is possible to perform parallel processing by connecting the computers in a network. However, this type of parallel processing requires very sophisticated software called distributed processing software. But, parallel processing differs from multi-tasking, in which a CPU provides the illusion of simultaneously executing instructions from multiple different programs by rapidly switching between them, or "interleaving" their instructions.

Generally, parallel processing known as parallel computing provides a viable option in terms of cheaper computing. This is because its idea time of processor cycles across network can be use effectively by sophisticated distributed-processing software in parallel processing computation.

End of Chapter Three of Section-One

Key Terminologies and Meanings

Terminology	Meaning
AC/DC	The description AC/DC refers to equipment designed to be operate on either alternating current (AC) or direct current (DC)
Apache License	This is a free software license written by the Apache Software Foundation. It is a free software licenses, which gives users freedom of uses.
Application Software	It is a package designed to help in accomplishment of some certain work in computer.
Bandwidth	The capacity, often measured resource utilization in bits per second during any communication channel. Example, connection to an Internet.
Buffer	It is a place, especially in RAM, for the temporary storage of data for printing or disk access in order to speed up computer's operation.
DASD	DASD (Direct Access Storage Device) is any secondary storage device, which has relatively low access time for all its capacity, e.g. disk drive.
Database	A database consists of an organized collection of data for one or more multiple uses.
F# Compiler	F# pronounced as (**eff Sharp**) is a strongly typed, multi-paradigm programming language that encompasses functional, imperative, and object-oriented programming techniques.
Gigabyte (GB)	Billion byte
Graphic	It is visual representation of picture, diagram, etc.
Hectobyte (HB)e	Hundred byte
HTTP	HTTP (Hypertext Transfer Protocol) is the categorized protocol and designation models of computer networking made for distributive, collaborative and hypermedia information systems. It is a webpage enabling computer program.
Hyper-V	It is code-named for the word 'Viridian'. It is formerly known as Windows Server Virtualization, which is a native hypervisor that enables platform virtualization on x86-64 computers.
IEEE 802.11 standards.	It is a set of standards carrying out wireless local area network (WLAN) computer communication in the 2.4, 3.6 and 5 GHz (gigahertz) frequency bands.
Intel	The largest semiconductor or microprocessor manufacturing company.
Interface	It is any type of point, where two different things come together, for example, what you see on the screen is the interface between you and what the computer is doing.
Interoperability	It is a property referring to the ability of diverse systems and organizations to work together.
Kilobyte (KB)	Thousand byte
Megabyte (MB)	Million byte
Open Group	It is an industry consortium for open system.
Open Software Standard	A Software producing standard that is publicly available and associated with various rights to be used by the public, and may also have various properties of how it was designed and made open to the public.
Open source	It describes practices in production and development that promote access to the end product's source materials.
Operating System	It is a set of instruction designed to act as a manager to other systems or programs in computer. OS is a program manager.

Palm OS	It is operating systems normally found in PDAs, e.g. smartphones, and was initially developed by Palm Incorporate.
Parallel Sysplex	It is cluster of IBM mainframes acting together as a single system image with operating system used for disaster recovery. For instance, it combines data sharing and parallel computing to allow a cluster of up to 32 systems to share a workload for high performance and high availability.
Precision	It is the degree to which repeated measurements under unchanged conditions show the same results.
Real-time	It is the battery powered circuiting, which keeps the track of date and time in computer even when the computer is switched off
Reboot	A process of refreshing the initial booting process of computer for the second time due to malfunctioning booting process. The computer command use in rebooting a powered-on computer is Ctrl+Alt+Del.
Serialization	In the context of data storage and transmission, serialization is the process of converting a data structure or object into a sequence of bits so that it can be stored in a file, a memory buffer, or transmitted across a network for use.
SUS	SUS (Single UNIX Specification) is the collective name of a family of standards for computer operating systems to qualify for the name "UNIX".
Terabyte (TB)	Trillion byte
Virtual machines	It is a software implementation of computer that executes programs like a physical machine.
Wi-Fi	It is a trademark of the Wi-Fi Alliance, which manufacturers may use as a brand to certify their products or devices based on IEEE 802.11 standards.
Window CE	Known as Windows Embedded Compact. It is an operating system developed by Microsoft for minimalistic computers and embedded systems.
Workstation	It is referring to a mainframe computer terminal or a PC connected to a network.

Objectives Assessment of Chapter Three

1. Examine yourself whether you perfectly achieved the objectives of this last Chapter, if not, read it again. However, if you have any question regarding to what you have learnt, visit **www.onlineworkdata.com**.

2. If you are successful, move to the Chapter four.

"The Components of Computer"

Chapter Four of Section-One
The Common Components of Computer

INTRODUCTION

The field of computer science and engineering involves the activities of designing computer, together with the hardware and software that make up its components. It is the integration of the components that make computers to carry out commands based on requested instructions. In this manner, every computer can receive information as data input through an executing component, processes the information, therefore, displays or produces the expected result as output. This can be achieved base on its integrated components, which functions in sequential and randomly order. For instance, each component is dedicated to perform a (or some) specific function(s), and it is the aggregate functions of the components that make computer a superlative machine. For category, these components are categorized into hardware and software. The hardware components are the physical, electronic, and mechanical components of the computer. They are classified into two forms; *locational classification of hardware*, and *equipment classification of hardware*. The locational classification of hardware grouped hardware into external and internal hardware. In this aspect, hardware such as monitor, mouse, keyboard, printer are examples of external hardware, while hardware like motherboard, RAM, power-pack are examples of internal hardware. In the other hand, equipment classification of hardware grouped hardware into *main, peripheral, accessory, networking, and consumable hardware*. In the other hand, software is a set of programs designed to make computer to be operative and capable in performing tasks. The software is grouped into *operating system software, programmable software, Accessory software,* and *application (program) software.* However, for the method of our learning, this Chapter briefly teaches the hardware and software components of computer based on their common components. So for the learning benefits, achieving the objectives of this Chapter will help in CAplus-2, which is an advance book written for further study of "Hardware and Software". Truly, students who studied the CAplus-2 will be intensely exposed to Hardware and Software Repair and Maintenance written in CAplus-4.

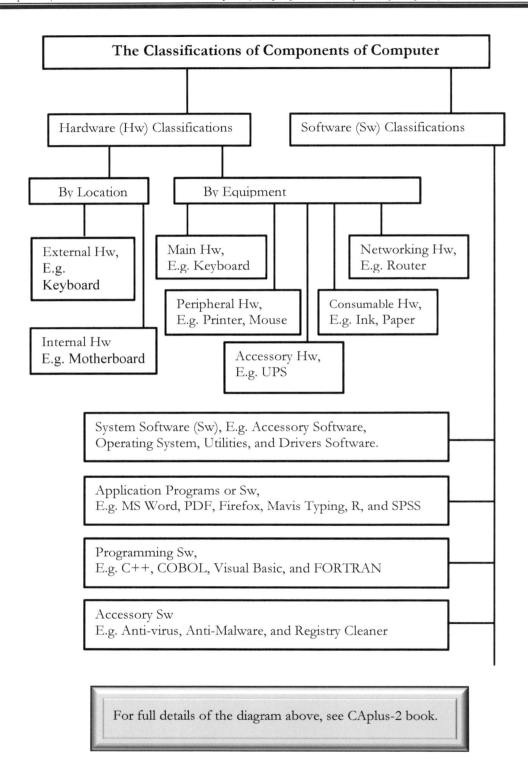

THE HARDWARE

By hardware of computer, we are referring to all the physical, electronic, and mechanical components of computer that we can see and touch.

The Main Hardware

As we mentioned in our introductory page, the main hardware of computer are the monitor, keyboard and system unit that have their respective individual components. In some computers like desktop, they are built separately, while in most computers like PDAs or Laptop, they are not detachable, but are all coupled as different individual units.

Many people erroneously are referring computer *System Unit (SU)* as the *Central Processing Unit (CPU)*. Although, as each of the main hardware exists in unit forms, for instance, the monitor been called Visual Display Unit, the Keyboard as Keyboard Unit, so also the System Unit exists. The system unit functioning as the processing-house of the computer is the connection centre for all computer hardware and software. This is why it (the system unit) functions as the CPU, but not actually the CPU. The CPU having its own components such as Registers, Controller Circuitry, and ALU *(Arithmetic/Logical Unit)* is been referred as the 'brain' of the computer. It is a motherboard sub-component and responsible for the processing functions of computer.

The *Monitor* known also as *Visual Display Unit (VDU)* is the output hardware that displays the information computer user is working with via a screen. It varies in sizes and colour outputs. For instance, depending on the screen contents, a monitor can be a monochrome (one-colour) or graphic (multi-colours) output display monitor. Moreover, no matter their size differences, monitors are classified into *traditional* and *non-traditional (modern) monitors.* They have their various display devices such as *CRT* (cathode ray tube), *TFT-LCD* (thin film transistor-liquid crystal display), and *PDP* (plasma display panel). These display devices constitute some elements and electronic components that produced the display capacity, which varies among them.

The *Keyboard* is an input device used to "enter or type" text and numbers into computer. Apart from "typing of texts", it is also used for keystroke-shortcuts, access menus, and give commands to the operating system of computer. The keys are arranged into Alphabetical, Numerical, Arrow, Function, Computer, and Status indicator signal keys. For general layout, keyboards are named in the pattern of the first six keys, whereby we have QWERTY, ABCDE, XPeRT, Dvorak and AZERTY, which is named for the first keys in their pattern. For example, Nigeria, USA, and UK are using QWERTY keyboard.

A Desktop Computer

The Peripheral Hardware

The peripheral hardware are those physical computer components, which enhance the proper functions of computer. They are directly connected to the computer (or the system unit) in order to help the operations of the computer. Unlike the main hardware without any of them, the computer will still function. Examples are Mouse, Scanner, and Printer.

The *Mouse* is a pointing device that functions by detecting two-dimensional motion relative to its supporting surface. It is a relative pointing device because there are no defined limits to its movement and its placement on a surface does not map directly to a specific screen location. As a two-dimensional device, it is used to select items or choose commands on the screen. How it works, the user presses one of its buttons, and gets an output or result by clicking the appropriate button.

The *Printer* device produces a hard copy of documents stored in electronic form, usually on physical print media such as paper or transparencies by printing out the stored information on a hard copy of a document.

The *Scanner* is a device, which is optically used to scan images, printed text, handwriting, or an object, and converts it to a digital image as output via the monitor.

The *Computer Speaker* is the device that produces the sound output of computer. They are of external and built-in speakers. The external speaker has the feature to disable the lower fidelity built-in speaker once it is connected and ready-for-use in computer.

The Accessory Hardware

Like the peripheral hardware, accessory hardware also help to enhance the proper functions of computer. But by connection, while the peripheral hardware are directly connected to the computer, the accessory hardware are indirectly connected to the computer in their operations support. Examples are Uninterrupted Power Supply (UPS) laptop battery.

The laptop and subnotebook computers are typically powered by an internal rechargeable *battery* that can be charge by the use of an external power supply. The power supply can charge the battery and power the laptop simultaneously; when the battery is fully charged, the laptop continues to run on AC power.

The *UPS* known as flywheel power supply backup, it is an electrical apparatus that provides emergency power to a load, when the input power source, typically the utility mains, fails. It differs from an auxiliary or emergency power system or standby generator. It prevents uninterrupted power supply to the connected device, therefore, can sustain computer user to roundup work, or put the main power source in order.

The Consumable and Networking Hardware

The consumable and networking hardware are also hardware that facilitates the work performances of computer. The consumable hardware are those materials in which computer feed-on during its operation. Examples are CD, DVD, Printer Ink, Printer Cartridge, Floppy Disk, and USB Flash. In the other hand, the networking hardware are the equipment that support the functional system of networking computation. They facilitate computers to carry out networking functions. Examples of common basic networking and dial-up connections hardware are gateway router, Network interface card, and bridge.

THE SOFTWARE

By Computer software, we are referring to the invisible components of computer in which through instructions tell computer on how to carry out its operations. They can be classified as System Software, Application Software, and Programming Software.

The System Software

This is the software, which controls the internal functions of computer, chiefly through the operating system, and also controls peripherals like monitors, printers, and storage devices that are connected to the computer. In operation, it serves in the combinations of device drivers, servers, utilities and Operating Systems (OS).

A *device driver* is program software that allows computer programs to interact with hardware or device such as printers, sound cards, scanners, et cetera. It typically communicates with the device through the computer bus by which the hardware or device is connected. Indeed, drivers are hardware-dependent and operating-system-specification; so many driver programs that come as part of OS are what determine functions of the related devices. For instance, when connecting a particular peripheral device, the user often must load its relative driver into the computer in order to enable the OS accept the device, thus assign function to it.

A *server* is computer, or series of computers, that link other computers or electronic devices together. They often provide essential services across a network, either to private users inside a large organization or to public users via the internet.

Computer software and hardware performances required analyses, optimization, configurations, and maintenance for proper and enhancement of their performances. So utilities are the kind of system software designed to help computer in such performances. They are mostly referred as software and hardware computer tools, Utility tools, or System tools. For instance, every installed Windows OS comes along with these utility tools known as System tools, however, computer end-users can as well through websites; download a third party free or professional utility tool that will be suitable for their computers. For instance, clicking the *Start-Button* and *All Programs Menu box* in any of the Microsoft Windows computer will prompt the User to the "*Accessories folder*, which constitutes most of the computer utilities.

Furthermore are the Accessory software, they are software installed into computer in order to assist working software such as Application Software, OS, and Programming Software to carry out their operational performances effectively in their due operations, and without them, computer can still function. They are like utilities, and can as well perform almost all the works that can be done with utilities. Majority of them are developed by specialized software companies, which exist as Third-Party companies. In addition, all the anti-virus software are accessories, especially as they served for computer software maintenance. For instance, application software like Adobe Reader is an accessory software use to support desktop publishing. Although, most of the OS like Windows OS came with their own, but known as System tools or utilities, which we learnt on the above pages.

The Operating System

The *Operating System* is a set of instruction designed to act as a manager to other software in computer. As software, it runs on computer, interacts with computer user, manages attached devices like the computer hardware through BIOS (Basic Input/Output System), and provides common services for efficient execution of various application programs like Word Processing, Spreadsheet, etc. In addition, it acts as an intermediary between application programs and hardware in memory allocation, maintaining files and running of application software (or programs), supporting input and output hardware functions, and as well as server provisions. Moreover, without OS, computer will be useless. Examples are Macintosh, Linux, and Microsoft Windows System such as Windows 2000, Windows XP, Vista, Windows 7, and Windows 8. In this manner, Microsoft Windows System is a graphical user interface (GUI) component constituting of desktop environment that supports window management implementation and, provisions of basic functions and support to graphic hardware like mouse, keyboard, and others. For work usage, it enables computer user to work with several programs at the same time. And in this condition, each program is designed to run on its window, which is generally a rectangular area of the screen, as most of them (windows) have basic support of re-parenting to overlap each other or flip in pages with *'backward and forward'* buttons support.

Operating Systems for Smartphones

There are various Operating Systems (OSs) for Smartphones (i.e. mobile phones) just like that of the PCs. In PCs, the type of publisher's OS, which runs on a particular computer, determines the type of application software that can be store in that computer. For instance, in PC, some application software publishers or developers will developed or published their software into Windows OS, Mac OS, and Linux OS compatibility. This is to enable those who run different OS to use them (their software). Although, for incompatibility, application software that is compatible with a particular OS (say Windows OS), may not be compatible to others (say Mac and Linux OS), unless such application has a separate version for that OS. This is the reasons why software developers or publishers often produced their application software in the compatibility of different OSs.

Similarly, this character is the same to smartphones. For application software, in PCs we installed application software, but in smartphones, we installed apps, which is the same thing as application software. But, unlike PCs, smartphones use various types of OSs depending on their manufacturers. For instance, companies manufacturing smartphones often placed different OSs in them. Examples of OSs used in smartphones are Symbian, Android, Windows, Blackberry, Apple iOS, et cetera.

Symbian: This OS is officially the property of Nokia, therefore for any other company to use it in manufacturing a phone that company must take permission from Nokia, or buy Nokia over. The OS is of two types, Symbian ANNA and Symbian BELLE. Some examples of Nokia phones using them are Nokia C6-01, Nokia 603, Nokia 700, Nokia 808 Pure View, Nokia E6 (ANNA), and Nokia 701 (BELLE), etc. Moreover, the OS is very popular among Nokia dual SIM phones, and Nokia apps is available in Nokia App Store, which has auto-installation in some Nokia phones.

Android: The month of September 20th, 2008 was the period Google Company released their first Android OS called Astro. Just after stepping into the smartphones and other tablets market, Android gained immense popularity due to its beautiful appearance, opened-source featured, efficient working, and user friendliness. Like other app markets such as Nokia Store, Google Play Store was established to exist as the market where to get apps suitable for the use of Android phones (i.e.phones built-in with Android OS). Today there are millions of apps available for the uses of Android phones. The fortunate thing is that, these apps are been developed by software companies and individuals that published and uploaded them in the Google Play Store for Android users to buy or use freely. For types, there are many Android OSs based on versions. Like we stated above, the first Android OS was Astro, then in the upgrade of the version came, Bender, and since Google decided to name the Android OS upgrading versions in alphabetical order, then after Bender came Cupcake, Donut, Éclair, Froyo, Gingerbread, Honeycomb, Ice Cream Sandwich, Jelly Bean, and others. Today, many phones manufacturers have built their smartphones to run in Android OS, and such smartphones include, OPSSON D1, TECNO Q1, Samsung Galaxy Gio, HTC Wilfire, and others. Moreover, the business policy of openly allowing any phone manufacturing company to use the OS in phone manufacturing is called opened-source policy.

Bada OS: This OS is been owned by Samsung, and it is been developed for mid-range and high-end smartphones. Similar to Android, the OS is a quite user friendly and efficient OS, but with less or no popularity. Among the phones that use it, are Samsung Wave, Samsung Wave 2, etc. Although, it is unfortunate that Samsung did not promote it very well, and that is the reason, it is not popular.

Apple iOS: This OS exists on a closed-source policy as it is been owned by Apple Incorporate. It was first introduced in 29th June 2007 when the first iPhone was developed by them. By closed-source policy, we mean the owner does not allow others to use it in the same manner they are using it, unless on permission based. So unlike Android OS, which many smartphone manufacturers are using in most of their products (i.e. as of when this book was written), the Apple Company has not allowed other phone manufacturers to use the iOS in the production of their phones. So the iOS is only found in Apple smartphone known as iPhone, and Apple tablet PC known as iPad. Examples of most of the iPhones are iPhone, iPhone 2G, iPhone 3G, and iPhone 4, while that of the iPads are iPad, iPad 2, and iPad 3. Moreover, a good example of the OS is iOS 6.

Blackberry OS: This OS is owned by RIM (Research In Motion) and was first released in 1999 for RIM smartphones known as Blackberry. Like Apple iOS, it is a closed-source OS, therefore not available for other phone manufacturers to use it in their products. A good example of the OS is Blackberry OS 7.1 that was introduced in May 2011, and it is been used in Blackberry Bold 9930. It is very reliable and immune to almost all the viruses that can attack smartphones. Other examples of smartphones using the OS are Blackberry Bold, Blackberry Curve, Blackberry Torch, Blackberry 8520, and others.

Windows OS: This is the same to the Windows OS we are using in PCs. It is been owned by Microsoft Corporation, and stands as one of the most popular OS in PCs, but not actually in smartphones. This is because of competition. However, this is not the same since Nokia and Microsoft joined-hand. The OS has move with great popularity, especially in the production of Window Phones with Windows OS like Windows 7, and Windows 8. The OS is now user friendly, and very effective. Examples of smartphones, which are using Windows OS are; Nokia Lumia 800, Nokia Lumia 900, Samsung Focus, HTC Titan 2, and others.

The Programming Software

Computer Program is a set of instructions that directs computer to perform some processing function or combination of functions. For instance, for an instruction to be carried out, computer must execute a program, that is, reads the program, and then follows the steps encoded in the program in a precise order until completion. Prior to completion, a program can be executed in many different times, with each execution yielding a potentially different result depending upon the options and data that the user gives the computer. In this manner, programming language software is the software that usually provides tools, which computer programmers use in writing computer programs. The tools include compilers, debuggers, interpreters, linkers, text editors, et cetera. Examples of programming language are Visual Basic (VB), and **C++**.

A *Compiler* is a program software that transforms a source code (i.e. sourced language) written in programming language into an object code (i.e. targeted language). The most reason of transferring sourced language into targeted language is to create an executable program. Following is a linker, which is program software that takes one or more objects generated by a compiler and combines them into a single executable program.

The *Debugger* is program software, which is used to test a running program, and debugging of programs. But, some debuggers when running have the capacity of program modification rather than merely observation.

The *Text Editor* is a type of program used for editing plain text files. They are often provided with operating systems or software development packages and can be used to change configuration files and programming language source code. A good example is Microsoft Office Notepad.

Application Software

Application software allows end-users to accomplish one or more specific task. Examples are the Interswitch application software that runs the functional activities of an Automatic Teller Machine (ATM). Some business software like SPSS, Peachtree, OLAP, SmartDraw, Microsoft Office Suites and Applications such as MS Excel, MS Word, MS Access etc. In addition are, Database Management Software like Epi-Info, DB2, SPSS, and Oracle. Educational Software like KVerbos, Pocket Oxford Dictionary, Britannica Encyclopedia, Mavis Beacon Typing, PC Study Bible, and, generally others covering areas of works like Medicine, Decision-making, and telecommunication.

The Disk Drive of a System Unit

A System unit consists of a disk drive that enables the computer capable of reading, retrieving, storing and writing of data. In this manner, a *Disk is a flat circular piece of plastic or metal coated with some magnetic particles in order to be used for the storage of computer information.* In the other hand, *a Drive is a path or access by which storage devices such as disks use to retrieve, read, write, and store information on themselves via the supportive computer components.* For instance, the disk drives serves as a communication link between computer and the disks, thus function as the mean by which computers carry out their data-processing functions. For instance, a modern system unit can be built with disk drives like HD-Drive, DVD-ROM drive, USB Flash Drive, etc.

The DVD-ROM Drive known as Digital Video (Versatile) Disc is a removable media uses for video and normal computer data storage. It is located in the system unit and made for data *reading* on the DVD. In addition is Floppy disk drive is a removable computer storage device. Its drive (known as *'A'-drive*) is the access or path by which computer uses to read, write, retrieved and stored information on a floppy disk.

The Flash Drive known as USB (universal serial bus) Flash Drive is a drive that enables data processing activities between USB storage device and computer. A *USB flash drive-enabled* is called USB flash drive, and every USB storage device consists of flash drive that enable it to read, write, retrieve and store data when plugged into computer.

HD (Hard Disk) and HDD (Hard Disk Drive)

The hard disk known as local disk is an internal storage hardware that keeps data inside the computer for later use and remains persistent even when the computer is not switch on. In other words, it is called fixed disk, because it is not removable from the computer. On its location, it is been located inside the System Unit, as this prevents a direct access to it, which is not even necessary. It is measurable in gigabyte, and the size differs. For instance, we have that of 160GB, 500GB, and other sizes. In the quality analysis of computer, it determines the storage capacity of computer. However, this is quite difference from the HDD.

The HDD serves as a communication link between computer and the HD. So it is the path or access by which computer uses to retrieve, read, write and store information on the HD. In drives alphabetical names, its identification symbol is '**C:**' known as 'C-drive', while that of diskette is 'A-drive'. The drive features one or more rotating rigid platters on a motor-driven spindle within a metal case. The platters are mounted on the same spindle and can be used to write, store, retrieve, and read information in the HD.

It is the hardness nature of the platters been located in the drive that gave the name as 'Hard disk'. To read, write, retrieve or store data on the HD, a single platter requiring two heads is used to perform the data processing on the both sides of the platter. For instance, as the heads of the HDD moves back and forth, or spins around from one track (within the platters), it finds data either to read, write, retrieve or store on the hard disk.

The HDD can be grouped into internal and external form of HDD. However, the usability of external HDD on computer is limited to the number of free ports or buses designed with the computer. Computers are limited to number of free ports or buses, so external HDD are identified base on how they are externally attached to the computer.

The Computer Storage Devices

Computer Data Storage (CDS) is referring to the means of using computer components and recording media that retain digital data to store computer data over a period of time. This provides one of the most functions of modern computer, which is data storage functionality.

The purpose of computer data storage is to enable data retention both for personal and computer use, and as well to enhance the operational functions of computer in relation to memory. For instance without a significant amount of memory, computer would not be able to perform fixed operations. In addition, with a data storage device like USB Flash, computer data can be move from one place to another.

Indeed, it is necessary to point out that data or datums (plural form of datum) in this format are pieces of information that are processed by the CPU.

Types of computer data storage

The traditional division of computer data storage is primary, secondary, tertiary, and off-line storage patterns.

Primary Storage: This is referred as internal (or main memory), and CPU storage system where the operating system of the computer is stored. They are directly accessible by the CPU, which continuously reads instructions stored there and executes them as required by the computer. Examples of primary storage memory are the main memory (i.e. ROM and RAM), and the CPU storage devices like register, logical unit, and cache memory.

Secondary Storage: This is referred as external memory where our day-to-day usable data are stored externally. They are indirectly accessible by the CPU, that is to say, the CPU can only access them whenever they are externally connected to the computer. The computer usually uses its devices to access and transfers the desired data through the intermediate areas in the primary storage, and saved them into the available secondary storage device. Importantly, if the computer went off, the data stored in them cannot be lose. They are non-volatiles, characterized with the capacity of mass storage, and can keep data for a long time.

Furthermore, the use of most of the secondary storage device like hard disk and diskette require them to be formatted in order to make them "enabled-for-data-use" by the computer. It is after the formatting that computer will start their acceptance for data processing. For an example, formatting a diskette will enable the computer to read and/or write on it. At the point of the formatting, it will check the diskette for bad sectors, and build a directory to hold information concerning the files that will be eventually written on it. Good examples of these secondary storage devices are hard disk, flash drive, diskette, CD, DVD, Blu-ray disc, etc.

Tertiary storage: A good example of tertiary storage devices are tape libraries, and optical jukeboxes. When computer needs to read information from any tertiary storage device, it will first consult a catalog database to determine which tape or disc contains the information. Next, the computer will instruct a robotic arm to fetch the medium and place it in a drive for a reading. And when the computer has finished reading the information, the robotic arm will return the medium to its place in the library.

Off-line storage: This is data storage done on a medium, which is not under the control of a CPU. The medium is recorded, usually in a secondary or tertiary storage device, and then physically removed or disconnected. For instance, in modern PCs, most secondary and tertiary storage media are also used for off-line storage. In this aspect, optical discs and flash memory devices are most popular, and to a certain extent removable hard disk.

End of Chapter One of Section-Two

Key Terminologies and Meanings

Terms	Meaning
ALU	It stands as Arithmetic/Logical Unit, thus serves as that portion of the CPU hardware, which performs the arithmetic and logical operations on the integer representation functions of the CPU.
BD-ROM Drive	The BD-ROM Drive is the drive, located in the system unit, and used for *reading* data from the BD (Blu-ray Disc).
BIOS	This refers as the *Basic Input/Output System (BIOS)*. It is a boot firmware comprises in the motherboard, which enable computer to carry out its booting operation when powered-on, and as well as other functions relating to power and hardware management.
Buses	Buses are the hardware, which connect the CPU to various internal components.
Cache Memory	It is a special block of fast memory used for the storage of temporary data for quick retrieval. It is introduced solely just to increase performance of computer relatively to data processing. For instance, most actively used information located in the RAM and ROM is duplicated in the cache memory just to increase computer performances.
CD-ROM Drive	This is the drive located in the system unit, and used for *reading* data from the CD (Compact Disc).
Compiler	This is program software that transforms source code (i.e. sourced language) written in programming language into object code (i.e. targeted language).
Controller Circuitry	The controller circuitry is the primary functional unit within the CPU.
CRT	It is refers as Cathode Ray Tube, which is a vacuum tube containing an electron-gun (a source of electrons), a raster-scan technology, a fluorescent screen, and a phosphorous coating at the back of the screen with internal or external means to accelerate and deflect the electron-beam, which is used to create images in the form of light emitted from the fluorescent screen.
Debugger	This is program software, which is used to test program running and debugging of programs.
DVD-ROM Drive	This is the drive located in the system unit, and used for *reading* data from the DVD (Digital Video Disc).
Flash Drive	This can be referred as USB (universal serial bus) Flash Drive. It is a drive that enables data processing activities between USB storage device and computer
Floppy Drive	This is also can be referred as diskette drive. A diskette (floppy disk) is a removable computer storage device. Floppy drive is the access or path by which computer uses to read, write, retrieved and stored information on a floppy disk.
Integer Representation	This is size and precision of numbers of location or address that a CPU can represent.
ISDN	ISDN (*Integrated Services Digital Network*) is a set of communication standards for simultaneous digital transmission of voice, video, data, and other network services over the traditional circuits of the public switched telephone network.
Linker	This program software takes one or more objects generated by a compiler and combines them into a single executable program.

Microprocessor	A microprocessor is CPU manufactured on a very small number of Integrated Circuits usually just one.
Motherboard	This is the main circuit board in a complex electronic system, like computer. It is the most 'central' part of computer
PDP	The plasma display panel (PDP) is a type of flat panel display common to large television displays.
RAM	This is a form of computer data storage attached indirectly or directly from the CPU to the motherboard. It is used for temporarily data storage and accessing of data randomly.
Register	This is the temporary storage unit of a CPU. They are accumulator, program counter and instruction registers.
ROM	It is a permanent memory containing permanent program and instruction that cannot be erased, e.g., the manufacturer information of computer.
Server	This is computer, or series of computers, that link other computers or electronic devices together.
Software	They are the invisible components of computer in which through instructions tell computer on how to carry out its operations.
Software Update	This is usually a task of adding relatively minor new features to existing software or correcting errors (bugs) found after the software was released for use.
Software Version	This is an indicating number, showing an update level of already released software.
Storage Device	It is any device use in storing computer data.
Text Editor	This is a type of program used for editing plain text files.
TFT-LCD	The TFT-LCD is a variant of liquid crystal display (LCD) that uses thin-film transistor (TFT) technology to improve image quality (e.g., contrast). TFT LCD is one type of active matrix addressing LCD.
Utilities	They are System tools or software, which help computer software and hardware in optimization, configurations, and maintenance for proper and enhancement of their performances. Example, Disk Cleanup System tool of Windows OS.
VDU	It stands as Visual Display Unit, which is another name for computer monitor.
Windows OS	Windows Operating System is a graphical user interface (GUI) component constituting of desktop environment that supports window managers' implementation and provisions of basic functions support to graphic hardware like mouse, keyboard and others.

Objectives Assessment of Chapter One

1. Examine yourself whether you perfectly achieved the objectives of this last Chapter, if not, read it again. However, if you have any question regarding to what you have learnt, visit **www.onlineworkdata.com**.

2. If you are successful, move to the next Chapter;

"The Software"

Chapter Five of Section-One

The Basic Operations of Computer

INTRODUCTION

In respective of functional differences among modern and digital computers, there are many and certain operations that are basic to every computer. These include input-process-output operations as the most common functions, RAM control circuitry processing operation, and interval operations such as timing, instruction-fetch, memory-read, memory-write, wait, interrupts, and hold operation.

Historically, all the basic operations except input-processing-output operations have faced modifications-induced enhancement, and improvement in the general operations of computers. The modifications are as a result of technological changes in software and hardware innovation, and improvement. However, most modifications are sole to their respective devices.

INPUT-PROCESSING-OUTPUT OPERATIONS

This is referred as the beginning-to-end operations, linear, or sequential order operations of computer based on data input, data processing, and output executions. Computer in this form of linear functions, first, accept information as data via the user's input action, process the data with the respective external and internal devices, and finally, displayed the data outcome as an output. Although, input in this category includes bar codes, speech that enters the computer through a microphone and data entered by means of a device that converts motions to on-screen action. Processing can be seen as series of actions performed by the computer in order to achieve a task for producing an output, and finally, the output, which is the achieved result wearing the form of data or signal sent out by the computer. Take for instance, a student doing an arithmetic home work has carried out a logical arithmetic operation of 4-5+6-7+(8 X 9) on his notebook computer or scientific calculator, consequently got a displayed result of 70. The arithmetic numbers are the *inputted data*, the 'act' of producing the result by the calculating device is *processing*, and the *output* is *70*.

RAM Control Circuitry to Hardware Circuitry Processing Operation

This is an absolute internal operation of computer. For instance, once data have been loaded into a RAM, the first instruction of the data will be transfer from the RAM into the Control Unit where it will be interpreted by the hardware circuitry. The hardware circuitry is a group of transistors, resistors, and capacitors that perform a particular electronic function.

In this manner, circuits may be made of discrete components wired together or be built into a chip. For example, a chip may contain a single circuit, such as a video codec, or an entire sub-system with many circuits, such as CPU. So circuits are always hardware. Although, there is a "software circuit", which may be refer as a circuit designed in the computer and simulated before being physically manufactured. But, the input-processing-output operation that we first discussed is the main visible operations of computer. As we stated, it depicts the linear functional operation and the respective devices of computer.

Generally, irrespective of the form of operation, whether the former or latter, the followings are internal operations, which occur during all computer operations. That is to say, in all form of computer operations, they must occur.

Interval Operations: An interval is a period of time between one event and the next. In this aspect, an interval operation is an operation period between one operation and the next operation. This mostly exists in computer programs with sequential operations. Take for example, the RAM-to-control-circuitry, and Control-circuitry-to-Hardware-circuitry-processing operation. In addition, the operations 'if not all' include timing, instruction fetch, memory-read, memory-write, wait, interrupts, and hold operation.

Timing Operation: This refers to the ability to choose the best moment to do something. Computer is designed to carry out its functions in the characteristics of timing. At this point, it carries out a required operation based on the specific timing of the operation. Taking for instance, the activities of the CPU are cyclical (i.e. of repeating processes), and the CPU fetches an instruction, performs the operations required by the instruction, and fetches the next instruction, and so on. This orderly sequence of events requires precise timing, and the CPU therefore requires a free running oscillator clock, which identify the appropriate time of all processing actions. However, the existing events in the timing operation are instruction cycle, state, and clock period. The *Instruction Cycle* is referred as the combination of instruction fetch and its execution The portion of an instruction cycle identified with a clearly defined activity is called *State*, and the interval between pulses of the timing oscillator is referred to as a *Clock Period*. Generally, one or more clock periods are necessary for the completion of a state, and there are several states in a cycle.

Instruction-Fetch Operation: Computer operations also include the act of fetching instructions due to input made. At this point, the first state(s) of any instruction cycle will stimulate the act of fetching the next instruction. For instance, the CPU will issue a read signal and the contents of the program counter will be sent to the memory, which responds by returning the next instruction.

Note that, the instruction constitutes bytes, and the first byte of the instruction is placed in the instruction register. If the instruction consists of more than a byte, additional states are required to fetch each byte of the instruction. When the entire instruction is present in the CPU, the program counter is incremented (in preparation for the next instruction fetch) and the instruction is decoded. The operation specified in the instruction will be executed in the remaining states of the instruction cycle. Although, the instruction may call for a memory-read or write, an input or output and/or an internal CPU operation, such as a register to register transfer or an add registers operation.

Memory-Read Operation: In computer operations, memory serves as a place to store instructions, which are the coded pieces of information that direct the activities of the CPU, and the coded pieces of information that are processed by the CPU.

Memory is also used to store the data to be manipulated including the instructions, which directs that manipulation. For instance, the CPU 'reads' each instruction from memory in a logically determined sequence, and uses it to initiate processing actions, and if the program sequence is coherent and logical, in processing the program the CPU will produce intelligible and useful results. In other words, an instruction fetch is merely a special memory read operation that brings the instruction to the CPU's instruction register. The instruction fetched may then call for data to be read from memory into the CPU. The CPU again issues a read signal and sends the proper memory address, and memory responds by returning the requested data. Then, the data received is placed in the accumulator or one of the other general purpose registers (but not the instruction register).

Memory-Write: A memory-write operation is similar to that of the read, except for the difference in direction of data flow. The data flow of memory-read, features the capability of the CPU to identify and understand written data, signs, instructions, or symbols, while that of the memory-write is to accept the writing and storage of data. So the CPU issues a write signal, sends the proper memory address, and then sends the data to be written into the addressed memory location for the written process to take place.

For programs and storage features, the program must be organized such that the CPU does not write a non-instruction word when it expects to accept an instruction.

For the storage, the CPU can rapidly accept any data write up and storage in the memory. But, in most cases, the memory may not have large storage capacity to store the entire data bank required for a particular application, then the problem can be resolved by providing the computer with one or more *Input Ports* such as USB port. In this manner, the CPU can address the ports and transfer its data content in them. In addition, note that the addition of input-ports will enable the computer to receive information from external storage device at high rates of speed and in large volumes.

Wait Operation: The wait operation occurs in the processing activity of the CPU, and time response of the memory to receive read-instruction from the CPU. Here, the clock period determines the timing of all processing activity. The speed of the processing cycle (i.e. the processing repeat of the CPU), however, is limited by the memory's access-time. So once the CPU has sent a read-address to the memory, it cannot proceed until the memory has had time to respond the read-address. This signifies that the CPU has to 'wait' until the memory respond to the read-address before its (CPU) processing activity will take place.

Although, most memories are capable of responding much faster than the processing cycle requires, while some may be slower than the processing cycle requires. This caused the 'wait' operation to be referred as memory synchronization.

The synchronization process exists between the memory's access-time function, and the CPU processing activities. So the CPU is made to wait for synchronization provision, which permits the memory to request a "Wait State". For instance, when the memory receives a read or write enables signal, it places a request signal on the CPU's READY line, causing the CPU to idle temporarily. After the memory has had time to respond, it frees the CPU's READY line, and the instruction cycle proceeds.

Interrupts Operation: The provisions of an interrupt operation are to enable a partnered relationship between the CPU and its depended devices, including to improve the performances of the CPU by making it more efficient in carrying out its functions. For instance, consider the case of computer that is processing a large volume of data, portioned to be an output to a printer, the CPU will be prompt to output the data through the printer, but either in random or sequential page order. So in the printing process; after the startup printing, the CPU could then remain idle waiting until the printer can accept the next data for another printout. However, assuming the CPU is on the action of running a particular program as the printing process is on, it will be that when the printer is ready to accept the next data for printing, it can request an interrupt, and when the CPU acknowledges the interrupt, it will suspend the main program execution, and automatically branches to a routine that will output the next data through the printer, and after the data is outputted, the CPU continues with the main program execution.

Hold Operation: This operation is necessary to prevent a role conflict between CPU and some peripheral hardware in the operations of DMA (Direct Memory Access)-enabled. For instance, in ordinary input-processing-output operation, the CPU itself supervises the entire data transferred, and information to be placed in the memory will be transferred from the input device to the CPU, and then from the CPU to the designated memory location. In similar way, information that goes from memory to output devices also will pass via the CPU. But, some peripheral devices are capable of transferring information to (or from) the memory much faster, than the rate at which the CPU itself can accomplish the transfer. So from the nature of computer, if any appreciable quantity of data must be transferred to (or from) any device during the input-processing-output, such peripheral device (if available), will be responsible to act as the intermediary provider, due to the fact that it will transfer the data faster than the CPU. So the CPU must temporarily suspend its operation during such transfer in order to prevent conflicts that would arise if it (the CPU) and the peripheral device attempt to access the memory simultaneously, and this is where the 'Hold' operation will emerge.

INPUT-PROCESSING-OUTPUT DEVICES

By computer device, we are referring to any computer appliance designed for a particular purpose of computer function. In this manner, input-processing-output devices are grouped according to their specialized operational bases. Therefore, we have input, processing, and output computer operational devices. These devices in computer science are pieces of hardware that are used for both providing information to the computer, processing and receiving the information from it. However, most devices require the installation of software routines called device drivers, which allow the computer to transmit and receive information to the device, and from the device respectively. Good examples of these drivers are webcam driver, USB driver, keyboard, joysticks, mouse, and light-pen driver.

Input Devices

These devices are called input devices because they are used in inputting data from the user to the computer. Some input devices are physically directly connected to the computer, while some can be physically indirectly connected. However, some are not physically connected, but functions with electromagnetic waveIn addition, the devices are characterised according to their input method functions such as pointing, graphic, direct, and automation, thus grouping the various computer input devices into pointing-input-devices (PID), graphic-input-devices (GID), direct-input-devices (DID), and source-data-automation (SDA). . Generally, most of them are third party made products. For instance, computer manufactured by IBM can as well accept the use of Mice (i.e. plural of mouse) produced by a third party firm like HP.

Pointing-Input-Devices (PID): These devices are referred as PID because they have the nature of simply-point-to-a-selection-for-action. They include mouse, touch-screen, etc.

Mouse: This is pointing device that functions by detecting two-dimensional motion relative to its supporting surface. It is usually place on the desk where the computer sits. For data input, by holding and moving it with the hand will allow the user to reposition the pointer, or cursor, which is an indicator on the screen that shows where the next interaction with the computer can take place. In particular, a mouse button is often used to click on an icon, which is a pictorial symbol on a screen. So we can communicate or input a command into the computer by pressing a button on top of the mouse.

Expressed below are how we can input data into the computer with use of a mouse:

- <u>By Pointing:</u> Pointing to an item means to move the mouse pointer so that it will be touching the item.

- <u>Clicking:</u> Point to the item, then tap (press and release) the left mouse button.

- <u>Double-clicking:</u> Point to the item, and tap the left mouse button twice in rapid succession - click-click as fast as one can.

- <u>Right-clicking:</u> Point to the item, then taps the mouse button on the right.

- <u>Dragging:</u> Point to an item, and then hold down the left mouse button as you move the mouse. To *drop* the item, release the left mouse button.

- <u>Right-dragging:</u> Point to an item, then hold down the right mouse button as you move the mouse. To *drop* the item, release the right mouse button.

Trackball: A trackball is used instead of computer mouse. It is computer pointing device consisting of a freely rotating ball in a socket with sensors that translate its rotation into movements of an on-screen cursor. It is always found on laptop. One can use it to play a video game. By functioning like an upside-down mouse, one can roll the ball directly with his/her hand in order to input data to the computer.

Touch-Screens: This is computer screen operated by touching. It is an input device that allows a user to choose options and commands on computer by touching the screen with a finger. One way of getting input directly from the source is to have a human finger-tap simply point to a screen selection. The edges of the monitor of a touch screen emit horizontal and vertical beams of light that criss-cross the screen. When a finger touches the screen, the interrupted light beams can pinpoint the location selected on the screen, thus accept the touched action as command. Most smartphones are built with touch-screen input data device.

Graphic-Input-Devices (GID): These devices are refers as GID because they are used for graphic work in computer. They include mouse, trackball, touch-screen, light pen, digitizing tablets, et cetera. For instance, the mouse by one of its technique can be used by the user to resize image size, moves image to a new place within the active desktop environment, and others. In addition, for direct interaction with the computer screen, the light pen is ideal. It is versatile enough to modify screen graphics or make a menu selection-that is, to choose from a list of activity choices on the screen. It has a light-sensitive cell at one end, for instance, when a user places it against the screen, it closes a photoelectric circuit that pinpoints the spot the pen is touching, and this tells the computer where to enter or modify pictures or data on the screen. Furthermore, is the joystick, which is a lever controlling cursor or hand-held control stick that allows computer game player to control the movements of a cursor on computer screen or a symbol in a video game.

Direct-Input-Devices (DIDs):   Most DIDs are magnetic disk, floppy diskette, flash drive and others, which can run the process where they are to serve as source document to computer. In this process, an existing "stored or saved data" in the device, say flash drive can transfer "saved data" into the computer via a compatible port. How it works, a user is just to insert the compatible device to the compatible port, then run the normal procedures (if any) as the data input will take place. In addition, the most common DID is the keyboard, which we have described in Chapter one. Using the keyboard as DID has its configuration with the computer. To input data, a user needs to 'presses the respective keys for the data input.

Furthermore, another set of DID are microphone, touch-screen, eyes-looking, and punch card, which are also called data collection devices. Microphone is a speech recognition device, which is used for voice input. Here the computer accepts spoken word through the microphone and convert it into binary code (0s and 1s) for understanding. Originally, typical users of voice input are those with "busy hands", or hands too dirty for the keyboard, or with no access to a keyboard. Most speech recognition systems are speaker-dependent; that is, they must be separately trained for each individual user. The speech recognition system 'learns' the voice of the user, who speaks isolated words repeatedly.

For friendliness, experts have tagged speech recognition as one of the most difficult things for computer to do. Today, software is available to let computers take dictation from people who are willing to make data input via speaking. Example of such software is Google-Speech app available for use in android Smartphones.

Another type is data collection via "direct looking" to computer. Here, users delivered input to computer by simply looking at the computer, and the computer will capture the look data as a source. How it works, the principles are reminiscent of making a screen selection by touching the screen with the finger, then the electrodes attached to the skin around the eyes will respond to the movement of the eye-muscles, which will produce tiny electric signals when they contract, and the signals are read by the computer system, which determines the location on the screen where the user is looking. However, this type of data collection is not yet common in PCs, but available in smartphones like Android. For instance, an Android smartphone like OPSSON D1 has a security feature whereby it only accepts a programmed face for desktop screen unlocking.

Source Data Automation: Although, this is another form of direct input method, but of more efficient than other means of data input. It is more efficient because there is elimination of intermediate steps between the origination of data and its processing. This is best accomplished by source data automation, which is an input-processing-output means whereby there will be a use of special device to collect data at the source, as a by-product of the activity that generates the data, and send it directly to the computer.

The idea of source data automation is to eliminate keying, thereby reducing costs and opportunities for human errors. For example, transactional data are collected when and where the transaction takes place. So source data automation will be necessary to improve the speed of the input operation, and as well avoid human data input mistake.

But, for convenience, we will divide this discussion into the primary areas related to source data automation, which are magnetic-ink character recognition, optical recognition, scanner, bar coding, et cetera.

MICR: This is known as *Magnetic-Ink Character Recognition*, which involves a method of machine-reading characters made of magnetized particles. For instance, the array of numbers across the bottom of a bank cheque is an example of characters made of magnetized particles. In addition, MICR is often adds by using MICR inscriber.

OMR: This is known as Optical Mark Recognition. It is a method of mark sensing, where the computer senses marks on available piece of paper. This is technique used for the scoring or marking of certain tests, such as West African Examination Council (WAEC) sheet. For instance, after using an HB Pencil on writing an examination, as one shade a mark on a particular 'answer' in a specified box or space that corresponds to what the person thought as the answer. The answer sheet is then graded by a device that uses a light beam to recognize the marks, and convert them to computer-recognizable electrical signals.

OCR: This is known as Optical Character Recognition. It is a method that uses a light source to read special characters and convert them into electrical signals that will be sent to the central processing unit. Characters such as letters, numbers, and special symbols can be read by both humans and machines. They are often found on sales tags on store merchandise.

A standard typeface for optical characters, called OCR-A, has been established by the American National Standards Institute. The handheld wand reader is a popular input device for reading OCR-A, and there is an increasing use of wands in libraries, hospitals, and factories, as well as in retail stores. For instance, in retail stores, the wand reader is connected to a point-of-sale (POS) terminal that looks like a cash register, and when a clerk passes the wand reader over the price tag, the computer uses the input merchandise number to retrieve a description of the item, then a small printer will produces a customer receipt that shows the item description and price. Prior to the printing of the receipt, the computer will first calculate the sub-total, the sales tax (if any), and the total, and display them as information on the screen, and print the receipt out from the printer.

Scanning: An inexpensive way to get entire documents, pictures, and anything on a flat Surface into computer is by using a **scanner**. Scanners use optical recognition systems that have a light beam to scan input data and convert it into electrical signals, which are sent to the computer for processing. Optical recognition is by far the most common type of source input, appearing in a variety of ways such as optical marks, optical characters, bar codes, handwritten characters, and images. Scanners use *Optical Character Recognition* software, described above, to translate text on scanned documents into text that is suitable for picture managing application.

Imaging: In a process called imaging, a machine called scanner will convert a drawing, a picture, or any document into computer-recognizable form by shining a light on the image and sensing the intensity of the reflection at each point of the image. In this process, the electronic version or softcopy of the image can be stored, probably on disk, and reproduced on screen when needed. In addition, by made, scanners exist both in handheld and desktop models.

Bar Codes: This is a code number represented on the product label by a pattern of vertical marks, or bars. It is used in sending product information to computer. For instance, the supermarket product bar code is used to send data about the product directly to the computer. Each product on the store shelf has its own unique number, which is part of the Universal Product Code (UPC). UPC is supermarket industry agreed bar code standard, although, other codes exist. For how the bar code function, take for example, using a retail store wand reader, when a person buys, say, a can of drink at the supermarket, the cashier moves the product past the wand reader, the wand reader will identify the bar codes of the product, and use it to interpret the information, thus store the information to the computer. So the computer automatically tells the POS terminal what the price is; and a printer prints the item description and price on a paper tape for the customer. However, the bar codes does not contain the product price, but the computer can be able to identify the product price because the price of the can drink and its bar code have been stored as a file that can be accessed by the computer.

Obviously, the advantage of bar codes is that it is easier to change the price once in the computer than to have to repeatedly re-stamp the price on each of the product. It has been described as an inexpensive and remarkably reliable way to get data into computer. In addition, there are bar codes apps that when been installed in a phone, say Android smartphones, and they will be used in reading bar codes information from any place, where the bar codes picture is drawn.

Output Devices

These are the devices that displayed or produced out the achieved result task of computer. They consist of internal and external devices that transfer information from the computer's CPU to the computer user. Examples are computer screen, printers, etc.

Computer Screen: This is the major display output device. The screen, which is attached on the monitor of every computer, is often the user first interaction with computer base on the user's input. For instance, input made via the keyboard into the computer is causal to display as output on the screen. Although, as we discussed early, screens come in many varieties, but the most common kind is the CRT.

Speaker: Computers can also output audio through a specialized chip on the motherboard or via an add-on card called a sound card. Then users can attach speakers or headphones to an output port of the computer just to hear the audio produced by the computer.

Printer: Printers take text and image from computer and print them on paper. Unlike screen that produces softcopy output, printer as an output device, which is used to produce printed paper output, known in the computer industry as hardcopy, because it is tangible and permanent. Whereas some computer output capability is limited to letters and numbers, while others can as well produce letters, numbers, and graphical outputs. Besides, letters, and numbers are formed by a printer either as solid characters or as dot-matrix characters. Moreover, there are two ways of printing data on a paper. They are the impact printing method and, non-impact printing method.

Processing Devices

As we mentioned early, the processing device of computer is the microprocessor (CPU), which is being housed in the system unit of computer. It has the capability of receiving information, processing and sending it to various different parts of the computer. The speed at which it processes information internally is measured in hertz (Hz). For example, we have a Mega-hertz (MHz), and a Giga-hertz (GHz). In this manner, GHz is equal to 1000MHz, and the higher the GHz or MHz, the higher the processing speed of the CPU, vice-versa.

Nevertheless, there are various units of CPU families; these include the Intel processor family, the Intel atom, the Celeron, the Core-line, Pentium, etc. The Intel family was the first processor; their examples are Intel 80286, 80386, and 80486. Then came the Pentium, and the first Pentium processor was produced in 1993, it'has a processing speed rate of 60MHz-200MHz. Then Pentium Pro in 1995-1996 (150MHz-200MHz), and from 1997-1999 came Pentium 2 (233MHz-400MHz), Pentium 2 Xeon (400MHz-450MHz), and the introduction of the first Celeron that have better speed rate of 266MHz-2.8GHz. Then the development of Pentium 4 in 2000 with 1.4GHz-3.4GHz speed rate. In 2005, Dual Cores were developed with brands of Pentium D and that of Pentium E. Following this trend, in the early of 2006, the Core Line was introduced to replace the Pentium family. To compare, the Core line is seen to be faster and has a higher speed rate than all the Pentium family, including Pentium M, which is the highest among all Pentiums. This is the record as when this book was written.

End of Chapter Three of Section-One

Key Terminologies and Meanings

Terms	Meaning
Bar Codes	This is a code number represented on the product label by a pattern of vertical marks, or bars, which are used in sending product information to computer.
Hold-Operation	This is the operation, which prevent a role conflict between CPU and some peripheral hardware in the operations of DMA (Direct Memory Access)-enabled.
Input	A human action of entering information into computer.
Input Device	These are devices used by computer user to input information into computer. They are to be group into pointing-input-devices (PID), graphic-input-devices (GID), direct-input-devices (DID), and source-data-automation (SDA).
Instruction-Fetch	It is a process by which computer take notice of instruction or command, and act upon it.
Interrupts	This is the operation, which enable a partnered relationship between the CPU and depended devices, and as well improved the CPU performance efficiency.
Interval Operation	An interval is a period of time between one event, i.e. computer task and the next in computer operation.
Memory-Read	It is the process by which computer read information stored in its memory component.
Memory-Write	It is the process by which computer write information input into its memory.
MICR	This is known as Mark-in Character Recognition. It is a type of SDA.
OCR	This is known as Optical Character Recognition. It is a type of SDA.
OMR	This is known as means Optical Mark Recognition. It is a type of SDA.
Output	Result of input, which occurs after computer process information.
Output Device	These are all the computer devices that carry out output functions.
Processing	An action performs by computer, after input in order to examine entered information, and then produce output.
Processing Device	This is the Microprocessor, which process information entered into the computer, and release output.
Timing	This refers to the ability of computer to choose the best moment to do something.
Wait	This is the operation, which occurs in the processing activity of the CPU, and time response of the memory to receive read-instruction from the CPU.

Objectives Assessment of Chapter Three

1. Examine yourself whether you perfectly achieved the objectives of this last Chapter, if not, read it again. However, if you have any question regarding to what you have learnt, visit **www.onlineworkdata.com**.

2. If you are successful, flip to the practical activities page.

Practical Activities of Section-One

First Practical Activity

You are expected to visit a nearby museum and view most of our historical computers, but whereby you have no access to such museums, then alternatively take the below option:

1. Get connected to an internet or visit the nearest cybercafé;
2. Use any of this search engines: www.google.ca, www.bing.com, or www.ask.com;
3. On the chosen search engine's searching board, "type" for e.g. "picture of ENIAC/Inventor";
4. Select different options that the search engine may give you, then take a perfect view of our studied historical computers. You can print the softcopy of the pictures out as a hardcopy for further tutorial purposes.
5. If you cannot carry out this first activity, read "Internet Appreciation" topic in CAplus-2 book, it will put you through on how to run the activity.

Second Practical Activity

Our definition of computer is AEDPSM, proof that your smartphone is computer.

1. Get your phone (or handset) and hold it on your palm;
2. Answer the following questions;
   i. Is the phone an *automatic machine*? Carry out any operational activity, e.g. adding any name on your phonebook. Watch! Scroll your phonebook, you may found out that the registered name is automatically placed in alphabetical order.
   ii. Is the phone an *electronic machine*? With an appropriate toolkit, open the phone, look, and touch the motherboard of the phone, which is common to all electronic devices. In addition, observe other electronic features such as the integrated circuit (chip) of the phone.
   iii. Is the phone a *data-processing machine*? Carry out some operational activities, examples, arithmetic work with the calculator App of the phone or dial your network checking account balance via your network service code. You observe the phone "processing" the inputted data on whichever operational activity executed before producing the "output".
   iv. Is the phone a *storage machine*? Open the 'contact' dialog box of the phone via the 'menu' box. Click the contact dialog box, scroll setting and click on it, finally, scroll to memory status and click on it. You will access your memory status indicating the storage capacity of your phone and network SIM card, which proved your phone to be a storage machine.

      Please note that the method-used is not the same in all phones.
   v. Is the phone a *machine*? Check the phone, it uses electrical energy, (even some like Nokia E77i use solar energy), it has components, and it is repairable, damageable and need maintenance, just like other machines.
3. Computer can take simple decision of "yes or no", likewise a phone; Take an operation, may be deleting a name on your phonebook, the phone will demand a decision of "yes or no" from you.

Third Practical Activity

If you are a city dweller, you are expected to identify the institutions using most of our classified computers in their various centres:

Visit the following institutions below:

- a large hospital with computer equipment for laboratory work;
- a power/energy supply company;
- the operational control management office in a nearby airport;
- an extractive company specializing in crude oil drilling;
- a rubber plastic manufacturing company; and,
- any large cyber café.

Take these following steps to support the visitation:

1. Write a formal letter to the relative institution. If it is a group visitation, the visitation should be an expedition,
2. the letter should bear the reason of the visitation or expedition,
3. before the date of the appointment, on your jotting note, write down your questions: for instance "Sir, how does this computer (for example, grid computer) support the management productivity;'
4. dressed cute and arrived at the company premises at the appointed time with a copy of this book; and,
5. be courtesy in your questions and leave the place with a "thank you letter" that accompanied you to the place.

Fourth Practical Activities

You are expected to find out types of software through Google Search Engine.

6. Visit a Cybercafe, or make use of a MODEM and connect to INTERNET;
7. On the address bar of the browser, type *www.google.ca*, and press the Enter-Key;
8. On the search engine's searching board, "type" for e.g. "lists of Programming Software";
9. Select different options that the search engine may give you, then take a perfect view of our studied historical computers. You can print the softcopy of the pictures out as a hardcopy for further tutorial purposes.
10. Do the same search activity for the Hardware components you studied.

> **Note:**
> If you cannot carry out the fourth practical activity, read the "Internet Appreciation" topic in CAplus-3 book, it will put you through on how to run the activity.

Fifth Practical Activity

> ### Note
>
> Do not put away this book when all its objectives are not achieved.

1. If you have any comment or question, visit **www.onlineworkdata.com.**

2. If you are successful with the Section-one, move to Section-two;

"Building computer Career"

SECTION-TWO
Building Computer Career

Section Studies

The Section study is grouped into these career topics:

1. Information System Management;

2. Database Administration;

3. Computer Instruction;

4. Computer Programming;

5. Computer Engineering;

6. Software Engineering;

Practical Activities

There is an assignment for the section.

Objectives of the Studies

At the end of the study, Students should be able to:

- have the overview of the above listed computer careers;
- know their job training and educational requirements;
- know the personal qualifications required in order to be successful in their practices;
- know their potential, job outlook, and employment opportunity level.

GENERAL INTRODUCTION OF SECTION-TWO

Making a rightful decision about a particular career requires getting accurate information about the opportunities and occupations that career may provide. Like other similar careers, Computer as a career requires building processes, and in the pursuit, there is the need for accurate information in order to support decision-making. For instance, a person who wants to be computer Software Engineer needs to know its job description and review that describes the work activities and environment of it. In addition are the training and career education requirements, personal skills required, earning potential, the job outlook, and employment opportunity level.

However, it is unfortunate that many people are quick to pursue a career path that ultimately does not grant them the achievement of professionalism, personal, and financial aspirations. Due to this, in this Chapter, we focus to learn; how to build a career in some professional fields of computer. These include Computer Information System Management, Computer Programming, Database Administration, and others.

CAREER ONE

INFORMATION SYSTEMS MANAGER

OVERVIEW

Information System Management (ISM) is the application of information technology to support major functions and activities of either a private sector business or public sector institution. In undergraduate point of view, it is a multi-disciplinary major that focuses on the fusion of information systems, technology and business management for two purposes: the use of information systems to solve business problems, and management of technology, which includes new product development and enterprise management.

Although, the vast areas of ISM are adopted in business organizations, therefore to develop any part of it (ISM) that will address organizational needs, **Information Systems Managers (ISMrs)** need to be well informed in business and information technical knowledge. They must understand organizational structures, objectives, operations and financial implications related to these factors. This is to enable them communicate effectively with users of the information, and to develop systems that will support their needs.

They must remain update with evolving information technologies and a have a solid foundation of technical skills to select appropriate technologies, and to implement computer-based information systems. So they must be vast in knowledge relative to systems development tools and techniques, information architecture, network configurations, databases, and systems integration.

In the study program of ISM, the program requires the fundamental intellectual content of both Computer Sciences and Business Management Economics. Apart from the educational training, which is the primary development-base, specialized certification in related computer programs is also good. So to build computer career to the level of becoming an Information System Manager, students require good educational, effective trainings, and work experience to reach the height.

For educational training, perhaps first degree in Computer related career, and with Masters in Sciences (M.Sc.) or Masters in Business Administrations (MBA) being an advantage, but not necessary as the case may be in some recruitment. In addition to educational qualification is formal work training such as running some certification programs that cover practical training on ISM. To achieve this, there are many Technology and Information Management (TIM) Institutes for such training. In addition, developing strong interpersonal skills, leadership, communication, software, and business skills will help the person to perform very well in leading a subordinate, relates very well, have an effective communication, and coordinate activities with every concerned facet of the organization.

So in the emerging of many TIM Institutes, which run the certification programs of the ISM, many organizations or companies need the services of an Information Systems Manager in order to remain in ISM compliance. The existence of industrial competition has shifted greater demand use of newer technologies in recent years, so firms are to advance in the ISM especially as commercial activities are technological dependent now.

The Tasks of Information Systems Manager

- Maintains Internet support, and supervising security operations,

- Works in the planning and developing process of all implemental phases of computer activities. These include installing software and hardware, program designs, networking, and Internet maintenance.

- Sets tasks, delegate responsibilities to workers, and are essentially and provide updates in technology news and advancement to help the organization stay competitive in the industry.

- Create and manage project plans for information systems and technology projects,

- Develop road maps for the organization information systems and technology objectives,

- Meet with vendors to evaluate what information systems, tech-tools and products that should be used within organization,

- Keep executive leadership informed on status of information system projects and deliverables,

- Stay current with advances in information systems and technology,

ISM Career Training and Job Qualifications

To attend the position of an Information Systems Manager (ISMr), it requires some training in order to meet the standard qualifications. This is because an ISMr must possess the capability of heading a team, work, and manage subordinates in technical areas, and as well help the management and customers to understand the organizations release information in simple terms. So the person must have formal and education training in one hand, and for advantage, formal worked experience, including knowledge of some computer programs like MS Access, SQL, Java Script, et cetera.

For educational qualification, the person must start with at least a graduate degree in any computer related course, although most of the management may require first degree and MBA with a technology concentration or MSc. in information systems management. For example, below is an advanced coursework in MBA Information Systems program the person can do:

- Database Management Systems
- Information Systems Strategy
- Information Technology Project Management
- Systems Integration, and
- Management of Information Systems

And for certification training, some technical and managerial certifications may be required. Examples of the most common certifications include:

- Project Management Professional
- ITIL Expert Certification (for IT Services Management)
- Microsoft Certified IT Professional, and
- Oracle Certified Professional

Required Basic Skillsb

Leadership and Communication: These skills are required because an ISMr needs the ability to lead an organization in their information systems and technology pursuit. In addition, the person must possess the capability of heading a team or managing subordinates in technical areas, and as well helping the management and customers to understand the organizational released information in simple terms through effective communication.

Business Skill: An ISMr requires knowledge of financial and accounting management for project planning and budgeting.

Interpersonal Skill: Strong interpersonal skills will help an ISMr work with different workers and as well coordinate activities with them. These include top management executives, departmental managers, contractors, and customers.

Software Skill: Possess the skill to handle some ISM software such as Java Script, MS Access, SQL, MS Project Planner, et cetera.

Job Opportunity and Earning

Due to global information technology, ISM specialists have good opportunity for easy job securing, and salary earnings. They can work in Companies such as Computer Systems Design companies, Software Publishing, Data Processing and Hosting, et cetera

Expired Sampled Job Vacancy for:
Career One

Information System Manager
Energy Solutions - San Francisco Bay Area

About This Job

Energy Solutions is a fast-paced and innovative firm with 80+ employees and has recently rolled out an Employee Stock Ownership Plan (ESOP). We are seeking to fill a project manager position in support of Information Systems solutions for energy efficiency and sustainable energy programs. As a member of Energy Solutions, you will have the opportunity to work with a growing and dynamic team, regularly collaborate with external clients and internal technical staff on Information Systems projects, and provide overall direction and management of software-supported energy efficiency and renewable energy programs. This unique position is perfect for individuals with technical prowess who want to have an impact on energy efficiency markets and greenhouse gas reductions through our work for major California utilities and other clients around the country.

Daily responsibilities include but are not limited to:

- Collaborating with client teams and technical staff to design and implement custom software systems.
- Assisting with the direction, management, and quality control of Information Systems projects and project staff deliverables.
- Providing technical support to system users.
- Assisting with the management of project plans and budgets, revising as appropriate to meet changing needs.
- Compiling documentation of program development and subsequent revisions
- Reviewing and analyzing system data and product performance data.

Minimum qualifications:

- Bachelor's degree in Computer Science, Systems, Industrial Engineering or similar technical discipline.
- 1-2 years of client management experience in the software industry a plus.
- Strong written and verbal communication/presentation skills.
- Previous project management experiences including budget development and management a plus.
- Energy efficiency/renewable energy domain experience a plus.
- Development or configuration experience a plus (SQL, JavaScript, Python, Access, etc.)

Our BART-accessible main office is located in downtown Oakland, CA. Compensation is competitive and commensurate with experience. Energy Solutions provides an excellent benefits package including medical, dental and vision insurance, pre-tax contribution plans and an Employee Stock Ownership Plan (ESOP). Please email a cover letter with your available start date and your resume to jobs@energy-solution.com. For more information about Energy Solutions visit us on our website at www.energy-solution.com. Information will be requested to perform the compulsory background check. EOE.

Desired Skills and Experience

Python, SQL, JavaScript, Access, Client Management, Project Management, Software, Renewable Energy, Written and Verbal Communications.

CAREER TWO

DATABASE ADMINISTRATOR

OVERVIEW

Database Administration is the function of managing and maintaining Database Management System (DBMS) software such as Oracle database server, IBM DB2 database server, or Microsoft SQL Server for the need of an ongoing management. In this manner, Corporations that uses DBMS software often hire Information Technology personnel called Database Administrators (DBAs) to administer their database.

There are three types of DBAs, which are Operational, Development, and Application DBAs. The **Operational DBAs** known as Physical or System DBAs specialized on physical aspect of database administrations such as DBMS installation, configuration, upgrades, backup, restores, maintenance, disaster recovery, etc. The **Development DBAs** are into logical and development aspect of database administrations, such as; data model design and maintenance, data definition language generation, SQL writing and tuning, etc. Finally is the **Application DBAs** work with organizations that use third-party application software, for example made for ERP (Enterprise Resource Planning), and CRM (Customer Relationship Management). Examples of such application software are Oracle Application, Siebel, PeopleSoft, and SAP. So with tech-knowledge of application software, the Application DBAs will be responsible in managing all the application components that interact with the database and, carry out activities such as application software installation and patching, application upgrades, database cloning, data load process management, and others.

Moreover, the degree to which the administration of a database is automated, dictates the level of skills and personnel required to manage database. The higher the automation, the higher the skills and personnel required to manage it. However, database administration is a complex, repetitive, time-consuming, and requires significant training.

For organizational responsibilities, since there are three types of database administrators, the responsibility of a database administrator depends on the employed-type, nevertheless, the common tasks of database administrators include:

- Taking care of the database designs and implementation,
- Implement and maintain database security,
- Database tuning and performance monitoring,
- Application tuning and performance monitoring,
- Setup and maintain documentation, and standards,
- Do general technical troubleshooting and maintenance,
- Work as part of a team, and provide support to colleagues,
- And others not mentioned.

DBA Career Training and Job Qualifications

Apart from the fact that education training is necessary in the works of lives, college degree in Computer Sciences or Engineering is helpful in the learning of DB Administration, but not necessarily prerequisite in practice. In other words, career-pursuit in database administration does not mandate first degree in Computer Sciences or Engineering, rather a related certification program from the DBMS vendors; take for example, Oracle, Microsoft, and IBM companies. Although, most employers need those with first degree related to computer courses, but some may want those with area of specialty in database administration. Therefore, for one to develop career in DB Administration and compete strongly in its labour market, the person needs first degree and database certification. For example, below are some certification programs for database administration career development:

- Microsoft's Certified Database Administrator (MCDBA)
- Oracle Database Certifications
- IBM DB2 Database Certification

Required Basic Skills

Business Skill: For sufficiency reason, a DBA knowledge of financial and accounting management, including market research, and operational research analysis.

Interpersonal Skill: Strong interpersonal skills will help in terms of office relationship.

Software Knowledge: A DBA requires the knowledge of software that can be used in programming, web development, database performance and tuning, including database management and file structure.

Job Opportunity and Earning

Due to global information technology, there are jobs for DBAs.

Database Administrator
American Pacific Mortgage

About this Company

Since 1997 American Pacific Mortgage (APM) has been the number one choice for the most discerning branch managers and originators because we do what no one else can do. APM has a proven track record of helping hundreds do what they do best - get results. At APM we believe it is our duty to serve our employees and our communities by bringing tools and resources to our originators while delivering quality loans to our investors. Our Vision: We are the best retail mortgage banking company in America. We empower our employees to exceed customer expectations, and to enjoy professional and personal success. Our Mission: We support our branches by building value-based relationships. We provide superior resources through collaborative strategies and the power of volume. We are committed to the success of each branch and the community it serves.

Our Vision: We are the best retail mortgage banking company in America. We empower our employees to exceed customer expectations, and to enjoy professional and personal success.

Our Mission: We support our branches by building value-based relationships. We provide superior resources through collaborative strategies and the power of volume. We are committed to the success of each branch and the community it serves.

Job Description

The Database Administrator (DBA) is responsible for collaboratively identifying organizational and end-user needs and developing databases to meet those needs. The DBA designs, develops, tests, implements and maintains database systems and works closely with other IT resources to diagnose and troubleshoot application and database-related issues. The DBA performs database optimization activities to improve application query and report performance. Finally, the Database Administrator develops database objects, data integrations (SSIS) and reporting solutions (SSRS).

Our preferred candidate lives and breathes data, is constantly looking for ways to improve performance, security and reliability, and is eager to be part of a fast-paced, growing company.

Desired Skills and Experience

- Excellent written and verbal communication skills,
- Flexible and able to adapt to a fast-paced, high pressure, short notice environment,
- Experience in the mortgage or finance Industry (preferred),
- SharePoint Development Experience,
- Sage ERP 100 (Mas 200) familiarity,
- Adaptive Planning familiarity,
- Prior use of Encompass® SDK, Reporting Database, third party integration A PLUS.

Primary Job Functions:

- Serves as a conduit between the technology and lending practices of the organization, relative to reporting and data management.
- Develop database objects and structures for data storage, retrieval and reporting according to defined specifications.
- Implement and test database design and functionality.
- Perform database tuning activities ensure optimal performance.
- Interface with various line of business stakeholders to ensure databases are satisfying business requirements.
- Create new and/or modify existing SSRS reports.
- Design and develop back-end database interfaces to web and e-commerce applications.
- Participate in evaluating code and in code review sessions.
- Data custodian of all data across the organization

Required Skills:

- Strong analytical and problem solving skills; Ability to analyze problems and work from issue identification through resolution quickly and methodically.
- Technical Documentation Methods and Procedures
- Excellent verbal/written communication skills with both business and technology staff; Comfortable initiating conversations with non-technical peers within the organization, as well as the ability to translate business issues and requirements into technical solutions.
- Self-motivated and detail-oriented
- Knowledge of fault detection and resolution processes
- Strong skills in maintenance tools and best practices processes
- Ability to manage concurrent tasks
- MS SQL Server/ Deep proficiency with SQL Server
- Proficient with Microsoft technologies (SSAS, SSRS, DTS, SSIS, BCP, SQL, TSQL)
- Data Warehouse Design
- Demonstrable experience with database normalization.
- Mastery of database fundamentals, design, theory and technologies.
- Advanced understanding of relational database theory and practice.
- Strong ability to architect, design and develop enterprise database solutions.
- Strong ability to define, design and implement logical and physical data models
- Strong database performance and tuning expertise.
- Strong SQL development skills (Queries, Triggers, Stored Procedures, etc.)
- Knowledge of data, master data and metadata related standards, processes and technology
- Proficient in major development tools such as source control, ERD Design Tools, etc.
- A minimum of two (2) years of experience in a database development role.
- Experience writing T-SQL, creating stored procedures, functions, triggers and other objects.
- Experience with query plans, hints and joins.
- Experience creating indexes on a SQL Server database.
- Experience creating and following backup and maintenance plans.
- Bachelor's degree in computer science or equivalent experience

NOTE: This job description is not intended to be all-inclusive. Employee may perform other related duties as negotiated to meet the ongoing needs of the organization.

CAREER THREE

COMPUTER INSTRUCTOR

OVERVIEW

Computer instruction is an act of training individuals on the correctness and effectiveness use of various computer programs for business or personal activities. The personnel who carry out such act of instructing those who do not know about computer or certain programs of computer is called Computer Instructors.

For the training, classes are offered based on the program needs of the trainee or student that wants to learn, or based on institutional time management. The Instructors based on the software, which they can effectively handle, train the students with aim of teaching them on how to use them. For instance, most Instructors offer training on basic computer programs for business and individual uses, and such programs include computer appreciation, word processing, spreadsheets, databases and even some basic graphic design or web page design. The training may be of standard, intermediate or advance, depending on the student's need, and instructing-capability of the Instructor. For instance, in Africa, the most common standard instructing programs are Microsoft Offices Suites and Applications, including some professional Application Software.

For work progress, some instructors may move from business place to business place, providing in-office classes (training) to people in the office by using specific equipment that the office or business owns. For instance, some of them may work for local schools, college and computer training centres. Highlighted below are their common activities of computer instructor:

- In most cases, meeting with clients or students, and determining what should be taught in the training.

- In some management, the computer instructor may be required to prepare the training course outlines.

- Developing structured lessons to increase the student's ability to use the various programs and computer systems.

- Researching, learning and working with the various new programs on the application that will be in request for training.

- Completing follow-up evaluations, getting feedback and modifying programs.

- Providing some crisis intervention or support help for individuals that have taken the program but are having difficulty with some aspect of the training.

- Helping the management to maintain their computers.

Generally, the career of computer instruction requires a combination of the knowledge of computer appreciation, specialized computer programs, excellent communication skills, and ability to follow program new version updates. However, the requirement of academic qualification is not compulsory, but necessary for communication purposes.

Computer Instructor Type: Microsoft Office Instructor

To be Computer Instructor, for instance, in the application of Microsoft Office (MS Office) requires any level of education certificate, and MS Office certification, such as proficiency in the knowledge of Windows OS, MS Word, MS Excel, MS Access, MS PowerPoint, MS Outlook, and MS Publisher. In this level, the common tasks include teaching of MS Office from the lowest version to the most current version. In the computer training institutes, MS Office Instructors can prepare training materials, and train people according to selected, group or part of registered MS Office. Moreover, below are additional common tasks of an MS Office Instructor:

- Teach computer appreciation course,
- Train people on MS Office Suites, like MS Excel, MS Word, MS PowerPoint, etc.,
- Train people on MS Office Applications like MS Project Planner, MS Outlook, etc.
- Help the Management prepare students handout.

MS Office Instructor Career Training and Job Qualifications

There is no much qualification requirement, expect Certificate of Proficiency in them. Educational certificate is an advantage, as one who wants to be an MS Office Instructor has to be a learned person in order to communicate effectively, have good presentation skill, and other benefit of learning.

Required Knowledge and Basic Skills

Teaching Skill: MS Office Instructors requires teaching skill, as one has to impart computer knowledge to the students.

Interpersonal Skill: Strong interpersonal skills will help in terms of office relationship.

MS Office Suites and Applications Skill: Requires the proficiency knowledge of MS Office applications and suites, and their operational skills.

Knowledge of Computer Appreciation: Requires proficiency knowledge of computer appreciation course.

Job Opportunity and Earning

Due to global information technology, there are jobs for Computer Instructors.

Expired Job Vacancy for:
Career Three

Computer Instructor
Southeast Los Angeles County Workforce Investment Board - Orange County, California Area

About This Company

Private non-profit entity dedicated to providing skills upgrades for qualified employees in the manufacturing and logistics industries.

About This Job

Part-time Computer Instructor needed to teach Microsoft 2013: Access, Excel, Word, Publisher, PowerPoint, and others. Assist client's company in transitioning from MS2003 / 2010 to 2013. Training to be done at client's company site.

Desired Skill and Experience

Must be a power user in 2013, have experience as an instructor, and able to facilitate the transition from MS2003 to 2013. Instructor must reside near the Orange County CA area.

You are to the next Career type; "Computer Programmer"

CAREER FOUR

COMPUTER PROGRAMMER

Overview

Computer Programming is a scientific work of ordering computer on how to do certain things by giving it instructions. These instructions are called programs. A person who writes instructions is called computer programmer. These instructions come in different languages called programming languages. Examples are Visual Basic, and C++. For instance, most programmers used special software such as the aforementioned to develop programs, while, some used text editor (notepad) to write their program instructions.
(See page 64 for more about programming software).

In the manner of program development, programmers exist by developing the instructions and languages that computer can use in carrying out its operations or functions. In this aspect, the process of writing any program involves time. For instance, the time it takes to write a program ranges between few hours for simple programs to years for more complex programs, and many programmers in most cases collaborate in a team in the process of writing a complex program.

Programmers are categorized as either **Applications Programmers** or **Systems Programmers**. Applications Programmers develop or modify programs for a specific purpose, such as taking records of company's sales, while Systems Programmers work in a much broader field the development of programs, modifying network instructions and operating systems, altering of the instructions given to networks and other systems units in order to enable them communicate effectively with hard disk of computer. In addition, they (system programmers) have a fundamental knowledge of a system, therefore possess the capability to resolve programming problems that applications programmer often face.

Presently, the most common form of programming in the computer servicing industry occurs for the rising popularity of software packages. Here comes the **Software Development Programmers**, who often work with other specialists in creating either customized or packaged general-used software such as games, financial management, and other programs used for educational purposes. Although, most small scale business units are characterize to employ programmer-analysts who do both system programming and analysis. However, despite the pursuit of been identify with companies, many programmers work independently as contractors or consultants for companies that are in need of specialize knowledge in the areas of computer languages and applications. For instance, a company like bank, may contract an independent programmer to provide debugging services that will help them run any kind of management software application, and although, in such hiring, the contractual agreements may range from few weeks to more than a year.

The common functions of Computer Programmers include:

- By using technical language codes that vary according to the program's use, programmers can take the designs of software engineers and turn them into functional computer instructions that make up a program.
- Often, programmers have the capability of changing existing codes and programs. Although, when they do this they place comments into the instructions to make other users aware of the changes.
- Programmers run programs to test and re-test them for errors.
- They also resolve computer problems and logical tests within the system.

Computer Programmer Career Training and Job Qualifications

To be computer programmer requires educational qualification, perhaps bachelor's degree in related computer course or, at minimum, a certificate of a two years computer programming. In addition, gaining an entry into the organization can goes along with associate degree.

In employment trend, educational acquisition is a more common need among employers with a rise in skilled and specialized job candidates. Employers typically seek computer programmers with specialized experience in a particular area of programming and with first degree has an advantage. But, some of them (employers) preferred candidates with practical working experience and area of specialization in practice.

For skills, the need for a particular set of skills varies according to the different fields, whether it is in engineering, mathematics, scientific, or business applications. For instance, the emerging of different programming languages is creating a competitive field for applicants with their relevant knowledge, and in phase people with skills in a special language that involve such technical features as graphic user interface (GUI) are highly demanded. In addition, highly qualified job applicants are expected to have business and management skills, which together with other skills can be acquired through internships or other certificate programs. For instance, a system programmer is expected to have a bachelor's degree in computer science, and should be able to configure database (including Oracle, Sybase, and DB2) and operating systems within the phase of different organizations. Moreover, other skills which are required are problem-solving, technical, analytical, and logical thinking skills along with patience and creativity in designing better programs. The ability to effectively communicate in a team is also an asset.

However, amateur programmers just beginning their careers may work alone or within a team, depending on the difficulty of the project. Some kind of supervision is always required at first, and programmers should constantly modernize their knowledge of new technology through offered courses.

For career advancement, chances of growth with an aim of becoming a chief manager or supervisor, and probably to the point of consultant depends on the person's achieved skills and point of knowledge level in the programming world.

Required Basic Skills

Business skill, Interpersonal, Software Knowledge, Communication, Database Configuration Skill, Problem Solving, Logical and Thinking Skill, Creativity skill, etc.

Job Opportunity and Earning

Due to global information technology, there are jobs for Computer Programmers.

Expired Sample Job Vacancy for:
Career Four (i)

Computer Programmer
99 Cents Only Stores - Katy, TX, USA

About this Company

If you enjoy working in a dynamic environment, for a growing company, consider joining our stellar team of professionals. We invite you to apply online today. We are located 5 miles south of downtown LA, just off the I-5. We offer a competitive starting salary, a great benefits package and opportunity for professional growth. 99¢ Only Stores is an equal opportunity employer by both policy and practice and subscribes to federal and state laws which forbid discrimination because of race, color, religion, age, sex, national origin, marital status, disability or any other legally protected status.

Job Description

- Define specifications for software applications,
- Develop required code,
- Test to meet required functionality,
- Debug for errors and provide all required documentation for implementation of user requirements.
- Collaborate with business representatives on the design and development of solutions
- Assist senior 2nd/3rd level support with problem resolution and implementation for supply chain applications
- Work with IT Management to ensure all application development aligns with corporate goals
- Responsible for delivery of code that meets business needs on timely basis
- Maintaining/fixing, testing, and deploying of one or more enterprise applications to meet the organization's on-going information needs.
- Contribute to design and code reviews, regression testing, documentation, and QA to ensure top-quality software
- Remain current with development methodologies and practices

The individual must possess the following qualifications:

- Must have experience with supply chain development including Warehouse Management Systems, Merchandising, Order Management Applications and Store Systems,
- Knowledge of VB (Visual Basic) and net.
- Experience in application development and integration. Proficiency in SQL and Visual Studio and proficiency in SSIS, DTS, and stored procedures

Required Skills:

- Bachelor's Degree in Computer Science
- 2 months training with Supply Chain for wholesale retailer
- 2 years' experience as computer programmer in supply chain for wholesale retailer.

Computer Programmer Type: Java Developer

Java is computer programming language that is concurrent, class-based, object-oriented, and specifically designed to have as few implementation dependencies as possible. It is intended to let application developers "write once, run anywhere" (WORA), meaning that code that runs on one platform does not need to be recompiled to run on another.

Java applications are typically compiled to byte-code (class file) that can run on any Java virtual machine (JVM) regardless of computer architecture. It has been one of the most popular programming languages in use, particularly for client-server web applications, with a great number of developers.

It was originally developed by James Gosling at Sun Microsystems (which has since merged into Oracle Corporation) and was released in 1995 as a core component of Sun Microsystems' Java platform. The language derives much of its syntax from C and C++, but it has fewer low-level facilities than either of them.

The original and reference implementation of Java compilers, virtual machines, and class libraries were developed by Sun Micro System from 1991 and first released in 1995. As of May 2007, in compliance with the specifications of the Java Community Process, Sun relicensed most of its Java technologies under the GNU General Public License. Others have also developed alternative implementations of these Sun technologies, such as the GNU Compiler for Java (byte-code compiler), GNU Class-path (standard libraries), and Iced-Tea-Web (browser plugin for applets).

Java Developer Career Training and Job Qualifications

Career training and job qualifications for Java Programmers share the same with that of aforementioned computer programmer. However, a student who wants to be a Java programmer is required to specialize in the relative languages, especially C++, which is used in Java software development.

Expired Sample Job Vacancy for:
Career Four (ii)

Java Developer,
IBM-Dublin

About this Company

IBM Ireland Lab are looking for technically gifted, innovative and motivated Software Developers to join their Dublin Software Lab at IBM's Technology Campus in Mulhuddart, Co Dublin. Our expansive product portfolio offers opportunities within technology fields and solutions such as Social and Collaborative Computing, Smarter Cities, Social Enterprises, Cloud Computing, Mobile, Data Warehouse and Analytics and many more…. Equipped with the latest tools, technologies and architectures, you'll enjoy the freedom to write in and transform a number of related technologies across a variety of projects. This will include developing complex new and existing features, as well as working on feature implementation.

As part of a matrix organization with a strong mentoring ethos you are encouraged to excel within a team that promotes risk taking and rewards success. Our focus is on delivery, not so much on when and where you work, so you'll experience a level of flexibility that many other companies just can't offer. We have opportunities for Software Developers who have both front and back end development skill/experience. If you have 2+ years' experience in the below disciplines, we want to hear from you.

Desired Skills and Experience

- BSc, MSc, PhD
- Commercial development experience in Java and experience with Java/Eclipse development environments
- Experience with J2EE technologies
- Full software development life cycle exposure including design, development, test, build, documentation, packaging and support/maintenance
- Excellent knowledge of Web Development technologies and platforms. Strong knowledge of PHP, Javascript, CSS, HTML, XML, Smarty, AJAX, knowledge of JavaScript frameworks such as Dojo, jQuery etc
- Demonstrable RDBMS skills - DB2, SQL Server etc
- Experience developing in a cross-platform environment (Windows, Linux, Unix)
- Experience with WebSphere, Weblogic, Apache, JBoss
- Experience within an Agile environment
- Excellent troubleshooting skills
- Excellent negotiation skills
- Excellent written and verbal communication skills with fluency in English

You are entering into the last career stage,
please study with understanding.

CAREER FIVE

COMPUTER ENGINEERING

OVERVIEW

Computer engineering is a discipline that integrates several fields of electrical engineering and computer science. In other words, it is related to Electrical engineering and Computer science. In the study of computer engineering, for instance, we will learn about the hardware and software of computers, including circuit theory and electronic circuits. This shows that, it involves the development of computer hardware and software, therefore stands as a science of making computers and their parts.

For practices, computer engineers are always trying to make new smaller and better parts of computers. They usually have training in electronic engineering (or electrical engineering), software design, and hardware-software integration. So they involved in many hardware and software aspects of computing, for example, from the designing of individual microprocessors, personal computers, and supercomputers, to circuit design. This is why the discipline is address as science of making computers and their parts. However, this is quite different from computer hardware engineers.

The computer hardware engineers research, develop, update, design, and test various computer equipment that covered for example circuit boards, microprocessors, and routers. They also work in research laboratories and high-tech manufacturing firms. But, this is not the same with computer software engineers whose functions are to develop, design, and test software. For instance, some of them design, develop, construct, and maintain computer programs for companies. They can set up networks such as "intranets" for companies, perform new software installation and system upgrading for them, and as well develop application software that businesses and individuals may need.

Some areas of specialty in computer engineering:

Coding, cryptography, and information protection: Computer engineers work in coding, cryptography, and information protection by developing new methods for protecting of information, such as digital images and music, fragmentation, copyright infringement and other forms of tampering. In addition, for example, they also work on wireless communications, multi-antenna systems, optical transmission, and digital water-marking

Communications and wireless networks: Those focusing on communications and wireless networks can work in telecommunications systems and networks (especially wireless networks), modulation and error-control coding, including information theory. In addition are high-speed network design, interference suppression and modulation, design and analysis of fault-tolerant system, storage and transmission schemes, etc.

Compilers and operating systems: This specialty focuses on compilers and operating systems design and development. Engineers in this field develop new operating system architecture, program analysis techniques, and new techniques to assure quality.

Computer networks, mobile computing, and distributed systems: In   this   specialty, engineers build integrated environments for computing, communications, and information assessment. For examples, they perform shared-channel wireless networks, adaptive resource management in various systems, improve the quality of service in mobile and ATM environments, do wireless network systems and fast Ethernet cluster wired systems.

Computer systems, architecture, parallel processing, and dependability: Engineers working in computer systems work on research projects that allow for reliability, security, and high-performance of computer systems. Projects such as designing of processors for multi-threading and parallel processing are included in this field. Other examples of work in this field include the performing works of developing new theories and algorithms, which stands as tools that can add performance to computer systems.

Computer vision and robotics: In this specialty, they focus on developing visual sensing technology to sense, represent, and manipulate environment that can lead to performing a variety of tasks through gathered information. The variety of tasks will include improved human modeling, image communication, and human-computer interfaces, and as well as devices such as special-purpose cameras with versatile vision sensors.

Embedded systems: Computer engineers working in this area design technology for enhancing the speed, reliability, and performance of systems. For instance, such work like embedded systems are found in many devices from a small FM radio to the space shuttle.

Integrated circuits, VLSI design, testing and CAD: This specialty of computer engineering requires adequate knowledge of electronics and electrical systems. Engineers working in this area, work to enhance the speed, reliability, and energy efficiency of next-generation Very-Large-Scale Integrated (VLSI) circuits and microsystems. An example of this specialty is work done on reducing the power consumption of VLSI algorithms and architecture.

Signal, image and speech processing: Computer   engineers   in   this   area   develop improvements in human–computer interaction, including speech recognition and synthesis, medical and scientific imaging, and also computer vision development such as recognition of human facial features.

Computer Engineer Career Training and Job Qualifications

Career training in Computer engineering requires educational training, and practical training of some engineering software. For educational training, Bachelor's (B.Sc.) degree in Electrical/Electronic Engineering, or Computer related course like Computer Sciences is necessary. However, in some countries where certificate varies, like the case of Nigeria, Electrical/ Electronic Engineering, and Computer related course like Computer Science are in Ordinary National Diploma (CND), which is a lower certification, and Higher National Diploma (HND), which is higher certification are also acceptable. For some employers sees the HND in Computer Science to be equivalent with B.Sc. in Computer Sciences.

For job qualification, since, the field involves the application of computer hardware, and that of software, it will be good in advance level; for computer engineer to specialize either in hardware or software engineering, then follow up with the requisite skills, which include learning of engineering software relative to area of specialization, and if possible, attaining some professional certifications in the country of resident, or that of other countries. In addition, work experiences will also be added advantage.

Required Basic Skills

Business skill, Interpersonal, Relative Software Knowledge, Communication, Tenacity, Consistency, et cetera.

Job Opportunity and Earning

Due to global information technology, there are jobs for Computer Engineers.

Expired Sample Job Vacancy for: Career Five (i)

Computer Engineering,
Easylex Information Technology, Lagos

Responsibilities

- Analyze information to determine, recommend, and plan layout, including type of computers and peripheral equipment modifications.

- Analyze user needs and recommend appropriate hardware.

- Build, test and modify product prototypes, using working models or theoretical models constructed using computer simulation.

- Confer with engineering staff and consult specifications to evaluate interface between hardware and software and operational and performance requirements of overall system.

- Design and develop computer hardware and support peripherals, including central processing units CPUs, support logic, microprocessors, custom integrated circuits, and printers and disk drives.

- Evaluate factors such as reporting formats required, cost constraints, and need for security restrictions to determine hardware configuration.

- Monitor functioning of equipment and make necessary modifications to ensure system operates in conformance with specifications.

- Specify power supply requirements and configuration, drawing on system performance expectations and design specifications.

- Store, retrieve, and manipulate data for analysis of system capabilities and requirements.

- Test and verify hardware and support peripherals to ensure that they meet specifications and requirements, analyzing and recording test data.

- Write detailed functional specifications that document the hardware development process and support hardware introduction.

- Assemble and modify existing pieces of equipment to meet special needs.

- Direct technicians, engineering designers or other technical support personnel as needed.

- Provide technical support to designers, marketing and sales departments, suppliers, engineers and other team members throughout the product development and implementation process.

- Provide training and support to system designers and users.

- Recommend purchase of equipment to control dust, temperature, and humidity in area of system installation.

- Select hardware and material, assuring compliance with specifications and product requirements.

- Update knowledge and skills to keep up with rapid advancements in computer technology.

Qualifications and Requirements:

- Minimum of OND in related field

- 1-3 years of experience

- Good communication skills

- An understanding of the particular computer hardware architecture you will be working with

- Experience designing, coding and testing software

- Familiarity with software test procedures or scripts

- Experience building your own PC systems

- Understanding of different operating systems, including Windows and Linux, and how certain types of software will work with them

- Experience with device drivers

- Understanding of networking and security

- Understanding of the sometimes specialized software that is typically used in a particular industry

- Knowledge of programming languages such as C++ and other object-oriented languages.

- Strong interpersonal and communication skills,

- Ability to work in a team.

Computer Engineering Type: Software Developer

Like we mentioned above, Software engineering is a field of Computer science, concerned with designing and writing programs for computers. Software engineers that specialize in applications or/and systems software are engaged into software use in designing, constructing, testing, and maintaining applications or system software. For instance, various kinds of software like that of operating systems, network distribution, and compilers, which convert programs for execution on computer, are developed by them.

In the programming or coding fields, software engineers write instructions to computer base on line by line order; on how it will perform or be carrying a function or operation. They are also geared to tackle technical problems and hitches found in software. Following this, those in this area of specialty possess string programming skills. They are more occupied with the development of algorithms, analyzing and solving problems in programming than with writing codes. Furthermore, they work in order to change or modify software so that it will be of better quality for uses.

For classification, there are types of Software Engineering, **Application Software Engineering**, and **System Software Engineering**. The applications software engineers are engaged in analyzing user needs of software as well as designing, constructing, and maintaining computer applications software and specialized utility programs. In this aspect, various programming languages are used by these engineers, and they are chosen regarding to the required purpose for which computer program would be used. For instance, *C* and *C++* are the programming languages that are most commonly, while *Java*, with *FORTRAN*, and *COBOL* are used less extensively. However, this is unlike the system software engineers that are involved in coordinating the construction of the computer systems of an organization, maintaining, and planning their future growth. For instance, in a company, they coordinate the computer needs and demands by every department, such as ordering, inventory, billing, and payroll record keeping. They also make suggestion concerning computer system's technical direction, and construct intranet for companies. In addition, are works that need configuration, implementation, and installation of complete computer system. They may also be part of a marketing or sales staff, serve as the chief technical resource for sales officers, staff, and as well as customers. Lastly, may even engage in product sales and provide continued technical support to buyers.

Java Developer Career Training and Job Qualifications

The career training and job qualifications for software engineering share the same with that of Java Developer career in software engineering. However, a student who wants to have edge in the labour market as software engineer is required to specialize in either as application or system software engineer, attain some professional certification, learn the necessary software related to area of specialization, and gain work experiences may be through full employment, internship, or industrial training.

Expired Sample Job Vacancy
for:
Career Five (ii)

Computer Engineering,
Easylex Information Technology, Lagos

About this Company

Intergraph helps the world work smarter. The company's software and solutions improve the lives of millions of people through better facilities, safer communities and more reliable operations. Intergraph Process, Power & Marine (PP&M) is the world's leading provider of enterprise engineering software enabling smarter design and operation of plants, ships and offshore facilities. Intergraph Security, Government & Infrastructure (SG&I) is the leader in smart solutions for emergency response, utilities, transportation and other global challenges. For more information, visit www.intergraph.com.

Intergraph is part of Hexagon (Nordic exchange: HEXA B; www.hexagon.com), a leading global provider of design, measurement, and visualization technologies that enable customers to design, measure and position objects, and process and present data.

Job Description

- Provides consultation in one or more areas for the design, development and implementation of technical products and systems.

- Recommends alterations and enhancements to improve quality of products and/or procedures.

- Supports all internal activities and product development.

- Demonstrates knowledge in a variety of the field's concepts, practices, and procedures.

- Relies on moderate experience and judgment to plan and accomplish goals.

- Performs a variety of tasks. May provide consultation on complex projects. A wide degree of creativity and latitude is expected.

Will perform other reasonable and related duties. The Company reserves the right to change duties at any time.

- Experience in piping design or chemical plant design preferred.
- Working knowledge of Windows Operating Systems
- Working knowledge of 3D Design tools, AutoCAD in particular.
- Considerable knowledge of Microsoft .NET, C#, ASP and related technologies
- Considerable knowledge of 3D graphics software (IE: WebGL, OpenGL, DirectX)
- Familiar with Windows installations (WiX preferred and/or InstallShield)
- Needs a solid understanding of ObjectARX, AutoCAD, or other design software
- Familiarity with Agile/Scrum development process and working in a team environment
- Candidates must be adaptable to a changing business and customer requirements
- Must possess strong interpersonal skills, problem-solving abilities, and the ability to multi-task.
- Good communication and technical writing skills are required.

End of the Section-Two
Key Terminologies and Meanings

Terms	Meaning
CAD	Computer-Aided Design
Computer Engineering	This is a discipline that integrates several fields of electrical engineering and computer science.
Computer Instruction	This is a learning act of training individuals on the correct and effective use of various computer programs for business or personal activities.
Computer Programming	This is a process that leads from an original formulation of a computing problem to executable programs.
Database Administration	This is the function of managing and maintaining Database Management (DBMS) software such as Oracle database server, IBM DB2 database server, or Microsoft SQL Server for all need ongoing management.
Information System Management	This is the application of information technology to support major functions and activities of either a private sector business or public sector institution.
Intranet	The network which links computers inside an organization and ease communication among the various departments
Software Engineering	This is a field of Computer science, concerned with designing and writing of programs for computers.

Objectives Assessment of the Section

1. Examine yourself whether you perfectly achieved the objectives of the Section, if not, read it again. However, if you have any question regarding to what you have learnt, visit **www.onlineworkdata.com**.

2. If you are successful, move to the **Practical Activities.**

Practical Activities for Section-Two

First Practical Activity

Using the same format we adopted in our learning, use **www.google.ca** as your website search engine, and write a short note about Building Computer Career in the followings:

1) GIS (Graphic Information Systems) Developer

2) Web Developer, for example WordPress Developer

3) Networking Engineer

Second Practical Activity

> ### Note
> **Do not put away this book when all its objectives are not achieved.**

1. If you have any comment or question, visit **www.onlineworkdata.com.**

2. If you are successful with the whole parts, put it (the book) in your **Library**;

3. The Author has another book, Please see the last page of this book.

REFERENCES

Adebowale Onifade, (Article): **History of Computer.** Electrical Electronic, Department, Faculty of Engineering, University of Ibadan, Ibadan, Nigeria

A.K. Dewdney, **"On the Spaghetti Computer and Other Analog Gadgets for Problem Solving."**, *Scientific American*, 250(6):19-26, June 1984. Reprinted in *The Armchair Universe*, by A.K. Dewdney, published by W.H. Freeman & Company (1988), ISBN 0-7167-1939-8

Arthur B. Kahn (1967), **An appreciation of computer appreciation. ACM Publisher, New York, USA**

Ebbers, Mike; O'Brien, W.; Ogden, B. (2006), "Introduction to the New Mainframe: z/OS Basics.", IBM International Technical Support Organization, *http://publibz.boulder.ibm.com/zoslib/pdf/zosbasic.pdf*. Retrieved 2007-06-01

Edwin D. Reilly and William Leonard Langer (2004), **Concise Encyclopedia of Computer Science***: John Wiley and Sons, New York, USA,

Encyclopedia Britannica (2003), *http://www.britannica.com*

Get the facts on IBM vs. the Competition- The facts about IBM System z "mainframe." IBM. *http://www-03.ibm.com/systems/migratetoibm/getthefacts/mainframe.html#4*. Retrieved December 28, 2009.Hally, Mike (2005:79). **Electronic brains/Stories from the dawn of the computer age.** British Broadcasting Corporation and Granta Books, London. ISBN 1-86207-663-4.
Jackson, Albert S., **Analog Computation**. London & New York: McGraw-Hill, 1960. OCLC 230146450

James, Daniel (February 2004). **"Using Linux For Recording & Mastering"**. *Sound On Sound*. SOS Publications Group. Retrieved 2008-02-

Kahney, Leander, **Grandiose Price for a Modest PC.** Wired Lycos, *http://www.wired.com/news/culture/0,60349-0.html*. Retrieved 2006-10-25
Kempf, Karl (1961). **Historical Monograph: Electronic Computers Within the Ordnance Corps**. Aberdeen Proving Ground (United States Army), *http://ed-thelen.org/comp-hist/U-S-Ord-61.html*.Largest Commercial Database in Winter Corp. TopTen Survey Tops One Hundred Terabytes. Press release, *http://www.wintercorp.com/PressReleases/ttp2005_pressrelease_091405.htm*. Retrieved 2008-05-16
Lavington, Simon (1998), ***A History of Manchester Computers:*** **(2 ed.), Swindon:** The British Computer Society, ISBN 0902505018

Layman, Thomas (1990). eds. **The Pocket Webster School & Office Dictionary.**
New York, Pocket Books

Lee, Sunggu (2000), **Design of Computers and Other Complex Digital Devices**.
Upper Saddle River, NJ, Prentice Hall

Lumma, Carl (April 2007).**"Linux: It's Not Just For Computer Geeks Anymore"**. *Keyboard Magazine*. New Bay Media, LLC. Retrieved 2008-02-03.

Meuer, Hans; Strohmaier, Erich, et al, (2006), **Architectures Share Over Time** TOP500.
http://www.top500.org/lists/2006/11/overtime/Architectures. Retrieved 2006-11-27

Microsoft ® **Encarta** ® 2009. © 1993-2008 Microsoft Corporation. All rights reserved.

MLA Style*: "software." Encyclopedia Britannica. Ultimate Reference Suite*. Chicago: Encyclopedia Britannica, 2010

Morris, William (1980). ed. *The American Heritage Dictionary*. Boston, Houghton Mifflin Company, USA.

Nadel L.D., Kramer M.R., et al (1977), **A hybrid computer system for use in cardiology.** *Med Prog Technol* **4** (4): 185–91.

Nwankwo Stephen (copied notes, 1998): **Desktop Publishing Training.**
Laro Computer Training Centre, FH, Nigeria.

Paul Niquette (1995). "Softword: Provenance for the Word 'Software'".
http://www.niquette.com/books/softword/tocsoft.html. adapted from *Sophisticated: The Magazine* ISBN 1-58922-233-4

Phillips, Tony (2000), **The Antikythera Mechanism I.** American Mathematical Society.
http://www.math.sunysb.edu/~tony/whatsnew/column/antikytheraI-0400/kyth1.html. Retrieved 2006-04-05.Shannon, Claude Elwood (1940). *A symbolic analysis of relay and switching circuits*.
Massachusetts Institute of Technology, *http://hdl.handle.net/1721.1/11173*

Smith-Heisters, Ian (2005-10-11).**"Editing audio in Linux"**. *Ars Technica*. Ars Technica, LLC. Retrieved 2008-08-18.

Stokes, Jon (2007), *Inside the Machine: An Illustrated Introduction to Microprocessors and Computer Architecture.* San Francisco: No Starch Press. ISBN 978-1-59327-104-6

Techencyclopedia (2003), **The Computer Language Company**,
http://www.techweb.com/encyclopedia

Torvalds, Linus (1992-01-05).**"RELEASE NOTES FOR LINUX v0.12"**. Advani, Prakash (2000-10-27).**"Microsoft Office for Linux?"**.*FreeOS*. FreeOS Technologies (I) Pvt. Ltd.. Retrieved 2008-08-18.

Verma, G.; Mielke, N. (1988), ***Reliability performance of ETOX based flash memories.***
IEEE International Reliability Physics Symposium

Wheeler, David A (2002-07-29).**"More Than a Gigabuck: Estimating GNU/Linux's Size"**. Retrieved 2008-08-18.

White, Ron, and Timothy Downs (2001), **How Computers Work.**
6th ed., Indianapolis, IN: Que Publishers.

Windows 7 Ultimate (2009): **Windows Help and Support files**. Microsoft Corporation.

Supported websites:

http://www.antikythera-mechanism.gr/project/general/the-project.html

http://www.dictionary.reference.com

http://www.en.wikipedia.org

http://www.inventors.about.com

http://www.newworldencyclopedia.org/entry/Abacus

http://www.onlineworkdata.com

http://www.yourdictionary.com/computer/

Notes:

1. I made a tremendous search by going through many materials including websites, when writing this book, please understand that information posted on a website is subject for updates and removal, and therefore take note as this may affect your reference search.

2. Most of the books serving as references where downloaded as eBooks on PDF. You can go to www.google.ca, search for any of the book with its title or author's name, and download a copy.

INDEX

A

Abacus 3, 4
AC/DC 1, 39, 30, 54
Accessory Hardware 58, 60
Accessory Software 57, 58, 61
Accumulator 68, 71
A-Drive /Prompt (A:) 65
AKAT-1 34
Alan Turing 7, 12
ALGOL 8, 9, 13, 24
ALU 59, 67
Advanced Micro Devices (AMD) 37
Analog Chip 43
Analog Computer 4, 5, 12, 32, 33, 34, 35
Analog Data 20
Analytical Engine 6
Antikythera 4, 5, 12, 34
Apache License 39, 54
Apollo Computer 27
Application Software 11, 34 54, 61, 64, 93
ASCC 8, 12
Atanasoff-Berry Computer 8, 12, 40

B

Bandwidth 11, 52, 54
Barcode 50
Basic Programming 31
Batch 1, 22, 25
BD-ROM Drive 67
BIOS 62, 67
Bit 7, 13
Blaise Pascal 5, 12
Board-Level Integration 43
Boolean algebra 8
Booting 55, 67
Boot firmware 67
Buffer 1, 54, 55
Byte 13

C

Cache Memory 11, 13, 67
Castle-Clock 5, 12, 34
CDC-6600 9, 12, 45, 46, 47
C-Drive/Prompt (C:) 65
CD-ROM Drive 67
Celeron 44, 78
Charles Babbage 6, 12
Charles Xavier 5, 12
Chip 43, 44
C-Language 10
Closed-System 37
COBOL 8, 13, 24, 58, 108
Colossus 7, 12, 35, 41
Compiler 64, 67' 100
Computer Engineering 103
Computer Programming 9, 13
Consumable Hardware 57, 58, 60
Controller Circuitry 59, 67, 77
Core Memory 27
CPU 44, 59, 66
CRT 59, 67, 77
Cuneiform 4

D

Data 17, 22
Database 54
Database Server 48, 89
DB2 64
Debugger 64, 67
Decentralized Computing 50
Dedicated Computers 35, 50
Device Driver 61
Dialog Box 80
Difference Engine 6, 12
Digital Audio Players 30
Digital Chip 43
Digital Computer 12, 35
Digital Data 20
Directed Access Storage Devices 26, 54
Disk Cleanup 68
Diskette 18, 22, 65, 66
Disk Drive 65
Dual-Core 44
DVD-ROM Drive 65, 67

E

Earth Simulator 46
EDVAC 8, 12, 35
Embedded Application 50, 51
Embedded Systems 28, 35, 50, 51
ENIAC 3, 8, 12, 25

F

F# Compiler 39, 54
File Server 48
Floppy Drive 67
FLOPs 13, 43, 45, 47
FORTRAN 8, 12, 13, 58, 108

G

Geometric-Arithmetic P. Processor 11
GNU (GNU Not UNIX) 38, 39, 100
GPL (General Public License) 38
Graphic card 96
Grid computing 45, 52

H

Hard Disk 22, 65
Hard Disk Drive 65
Hardware 22, 57, 58
HB (Hectobyte) 54
Herman Hollerith 6, 12
Hertz 19, 78
Hold Operation 69, 70, 73
Hollerith Tabulator 6
Http 48, 54
Hybrid Chip 43
Hybrid Computer 36
Hydraulic 32, 33, 34
Hyper-V 39, 54

I

IBM-1620 49
IBM-7090 Console 24
Icon 73
IEEE 802.11 Standards 1, 54, 55
Information System Management 85
Input 22
Input Device 73, 79
Input-Signal System 23, 32
Input-Processing-Output 70, 73
Instruction-Fetch 69, 71, 79
Instruction Register 71
Integer Representation 67
Integrated Circuit Computers 43
INTEL 54
Interface 54
Interleave 13
Internet 54
Interoperability 1, 37, 39, 54
Interrupts 69, 70, 72
Interval Operation 70, 79

J

Jacquard loom 5, 6, 12

K

Kilobyte 54

L

LAN 10, 27, 49
Large-Scale Integration (LSI) 10, 43
Linker 64, 67
Linux 37, 38, 39, 62
Linux Kernel 38, 39
Local Disk 65

M

Mac OS 11, 62
Main Hardware 57, 58, 59
Memory card 18, 19
Memory-Read 71, 79
Memory-write 72, 79
MICR 50, 76
Microcomputer 12, 28
Microcontroller 51
Microprocessor 43, 44
Microsecond 19
Microsoft Windows 37, 61, 62
Microsoft's F# compiler 39
Minicomputer 12, 27
MITS Altair-8800 12, 27, 31
Mobile Computers 30
MODEM 20, 109
Monitor or VDU 57, 59
Monochrome Monitor 59
Motherboard 59
Mouse 60
MS DOS 10

N

Network 13
Networking Hardware 58, 60
Nomograms 32
Notebook Computer 30

O

Op Amps 32
Open Group 39, 54
Open Software Standard 54
Open Source Software 38
Opened-System 37, 38
Operating System 54, 58, 61, 62
Operating System of Smartphones 62
Optical Character Recognition 76
Optical Mark Readers (OMR) 76
Output-Device 77

P

Palm OS 55
Parallel Computing 53, 55
Parallel Processing 10, 13, 46, 53
Parallel Sysplex 1, 26, 55
PDF 61
PDP-1 27
Pentium 44
Peripheral Hardware 58, 60
Personal Computer 2, 12, 28
Personal Digital Assistants 30
Philip Emeagwali 11, 12
Pico-Second 19
Plasma Display Panel 59
Pointing Stick 30
Portable Data Entry Terminals 30, 50
Portable Media Players 30
Precision 13, 55
Prime Computer 27
Processing 17, 20
Processing Device 78
Program 22
Programmer 17, 22
Programming Software 64, 97
Punch card 7

Q

Quad-Core 44

R

RAM 13, 28, 51
Real Time 55
Reboot 55
Register 59, 66, 68
Registry Cleaner 68
Relay Computers 40
ROM 28, 50, 51

S

Sequent balance-8000 11
Serialization 1, 26, 55
Server 28, 39
Server Computing 48
Seymour Cray 9, 12, 45, 46
Siemens 25
Simulations 45, 46
Single-Chip 27, 31
Single Instruction Multiple Data 11
Single UNIX Specification (SUS) 55
Small-Scale Integration (SSI) 43
Smartbook 29, 30
Software 13, 16
Software Engineering 105, 108, 110
Software Update 68
Software version 68
Stibitz Computer 35, 40
Storage Device 66
Supercomputer 9, 12, 45, 47
System Software 57, 58, 61
System Tools 61, 68
System Unit 59

T

Table Desktop 29
Tablet 30
Terminal 22
Terminal Emulation software 22, 25
Text Editor 64, 68, 97
TFT-LCD 59
Third-Party software 37
Timing 69, 70, 71
Torquetum 5
Tower Desktop 29
Track Pad 30
Transistor Computer 8, 9, 12
Turing machine 7

U

Ultra-Mobile PCs 30
UNIVAC 8, 12, 25
UNIX OS 9, 38, 39
USB Driver 73
USB Flash Drive 60, 65
USB Ports 72
Utilities 58, 61, 68

V

Vacuum tube Computers 8, 41
Vector Processor 9
Very Large Scale Integration (VLSI) 43
Virtual machine 100

W

Wait-Operation 72
Web browser 30, 37
Web server 48
Webpage 54
Website 48
Wide Area Network (WAN) 10, 27
Wireless Local Area Network (WLAN) 54
Wi-Fi 30, 55
Window CE 55
Windows OS 61, 62
Wireless Wide Area Network 30
Workstation 1, 10, 11, 45, 48, 49
WYSIWYG 19

Other Available Computer Books

APP-XL
PLUS
APP-XL SOLUTION
PACK 1.0.0

APPLIED MICROSOFT EXCEL IN STATISTICS,
ECONOMICS, BUSINESS, AND FINANCE PERSPECTIVE:
FOR MICROSOFT EXCEL USERS AND LEARNERS

N. STEPHEN

CAPLUS -2

Introduction of CAplus

Welcome to today's class.

We are covering the following Chapter topics:

*Introduction to Computer
*Computer Hardware and Software
*Windows, Internet, and Computer Threat Appreciation
*Basic Hardware and Software Maintenance and Repair
*Building a Computer Career

The Hardware and The Software,
for advance learning.

N. STEPHEN

App-XL Solution Pack 1.0.0

CAplus-3

Windows, Internet, and
Computer Threat
Appreciation

for basic and advance
learning

N. Stephen

App-XL (Applied Microsoft Excel) in Statistics, Economics, Businesses, and Finance Perspective: For Microsoft Excel Users and Learners.

App-XL and CAplus Major Distributor:

CreateSpace Independent
Publishing Platform,

4900 LaCross Road,
North Charleston, SC 29406,
USA.

To Purchase or be a Distributor:
Contact the Author via:
www.onlineworkdata.com or visit **www.App-XL.com**

www.ingramcontent.com/pod-product-compliance
Lightning Source LLC
Chambersburg PA
CBHW041418050326
40689CB00002B/565